OASIS
Moments

POEMS, PROSE AND SONGS
for Inspiration and Encouragement

BY PAULINE LATTER

CW01334258

Copyright © Pauline Latter 2022

The rights of Pauline Latter to be identified as author of this work has been asserted by her in accordance with the Copyright, Designs and Patents Act 1988

This collection first published 2022

All Rights Reserved. No part of this publication may be reproduced or transmitted in any form or by any means, electronic or mechanical including photocopying, recording, or any information storage and retrieval system, without permission in writing from the author.

Published for Pauline Latter by Verité CM Ltd.

ISBN No: 978-1-914388-31-6

Design, typesetting, print and production management by Verité CM Ltd, Worthing, West Sussex BN12 4BG UK.

www.veritecm.com

Introduction to the Author

I was brought up in a Christian home but, although I was confirmed, I didn't have a really close relationship with God.

My two sons were born with haemophilia, a condition whereby the blood doesn't clot properly, and bleeds into joints, muscles and soft tissue are extremely painful and can prove disabling and fatal. Life was a whirl of trips to distant hospitals, long sleepless nights, and for me – panic, despair, nightmares, helplessness and nervous tension. My marriage broke up and I survived on tranquilisers and sleeping pills. Despite remarriage to a kind and caring husband, I felt very alone and I found a degree of comfort in reading encouraging poems by Patience Strong.

One night I had a wonderful experience with God that changed my life completely. I had been thinking about Divine Healing for the boys but God healed *me* in unexpected ways. He showed me how He saw me and the true meaning of Jesus dying on the cross for *me*. Not only was I forgiven but I now knew God was real, with me in every situation, and able to guide me and comfort me. I had such a deep peace that I no longer needed pills, have since experienced several miracles and many, many answers to prayers.

However, God didn't take me out of troubles, and life has been very up and down but, despite all my expectations, my sons have reached their fifties, I've got four lovely granddaughters and I'm still reasonably sane.

My poems either come out of my emotions, what I've learnt from Scripture or by looking at God's creation. Watching my parents come to the end of their lives brought new thoughts, and sometimes I just feel that God is saying something for other people. The songs were written years ago but I invite you to make up your own music as you read them.

I pray that you will find encouragement and inspiration somewhere in these pages.

Index

Poems

Lights in the Darkness 11
Cathedral of St. Etienne 12
A Psalm of Praise 14
Autumn Leaves 15
Born Free 16
Father's Love 18
Frustrations of a Sinner 20
A Winter's Tale 22
Grace 23
Hope for a Year 24
Creation Around Us 25
Journeying Together 26
Just Being – a Tree 28
Just Being – Me 29
It is Finished 30
My Helper 31
The Answer my Friend 32
Ode to a Stubborn One 33
New Beginnings 34
The Artist 35
The River of Life 36
Thoughts of Mary 38
Though Mountains May Fall in the Sea 41
Come Unto Me My Child 42
Glory to God 43

Hallelujah Jesus is Risen 44
God Loves Me! 45
In the Beginning 46
It's You and Me, Jesus 47
Father in Heaven 48
Will You Follow Me? 49
Close Your Eyes 50
We Praise and we Worship You Lord 51
Ring Out Those Bells 52

Letters (from)
Big Sister (Moses in the Bullrushes) 54
Cleopas (Road to Emmaus) 56
Cross-Carrier (Simon of Cyrene) 58
Damp Disciple (Jesus Walks on Water) 60
David's Servant (David and Abigail) 62
Doubter (Noah's Ark) 64
Elated Father (Healing of Jairus' Daughter) 66
Elisha's Servant (Chariots of Fire) 68
Foolish Young Lady (The Coming Bridegroom) 70
Happy Girl (Jesus Rides into Jerusalem) 72
Delighted Onlooker (Turning Over the Tables) 74
Judgemental Man (Woman Caught in Adultery) 76
Kidnapped Girl (Naaman's Healing) 78
King's Cupbearer (Joseph in Prison) 80
Egyptian Steward (Joseph and his Brothers) 82
Leper (Ten Lepers) 84

Little Boy (Loaves and Fishes) 86
Lost Son (The Prodigal Son) 88
Man with Good Friends (Paralytic on the Roof) 90
Martha's Neighbour (Raising of Lazarus) 92
Once-Blind Man (Healing of a Blind Man) 94
Pilgrim (Coming of the Holy Spirit) 96
Refugee (Mary and Joseph's Flight to Egypt) 98
Rich Ruler (The Rich Young Ruler) 100
Roman Soldier (The Crucifixion) 102
Sea Captain (Jonah and the Whale) 104
Secret Believer (Being Born-again) 106
Shield-Bearer (David and Goliath) 108
Tax Collector (Zacchaeus) 110
Taxi Driver (Philip and the Eunuch) 112
Temple Teacher (Jesus aged 12) 114
Wedding Guest (Water into Wine) 116
Witness (The Stoning of Stephen) 118
Wounded Man (Arrest of Jesus) 120
Queen of Sheba (Solomon and Sheba) 122
Zookeeper (Daniel in the Lion's Den) 124
Servant Girl (Peter's Escape from Prison) 126

Reflections
An Unwelcome Intruder 128
Blessings 129
A Mucky Place 130
God's Pleasures 131

Going Rusty 132
Lifeguards 133
Nature's Artistry 134
Unfit for Purpose 135
Our Seeds 136
Filling and Emptying 137
Our Shepherd Leads Us 138
Pecking Instead of Feasting 139
Unexpected Delights 140
Ready for Anything 141
The Bumble Bee 142
The Wind of the Spirit 143
The Narrow Gate 144
Trapped 145
Vast as the Ocean 146
On Board Ship 147
Instructions 148
Me First 150
Are You There, God? 152
Consequences 153
The Field of Lavender 154
The Lorryload of Blessings 155
Tuning In 156
The Lone Sheep 157
Trusting 158
Rejection 159
Running to God 160

Tears	161
Faithfulness	162
The Six-foot Hedgehog	163
The Rescue	164
Support	165
Riding the Thermals	166
Picking up Splinters	167
Overgrown	168
No-one's Useless	169
No-one's Hidden 1	70
Maintenance	171
Imitators	172
Fruity Blessings	173
Changing Direction	174
A Safe Place	175
A Right Perspective	176
The Little Lamb	177
Not the Gardener	178
All the World's a Stage	179

Lights in the Darkness

Looking from space at our world in the darkness,
Lights, big and small, shine all over the earth.
Only God, or a spaceman can see their bright sparkle,
Can see the big picture, can know what it's worth.

We, living our lives, can be lights in the darkness
Each time we are thoughtful and care what we say.
A kind word, in season, like apples of gold,
Can encourage a weary one to keep on the way.

We may feel that we are a drop in the ocean,
That our pennies are few and the need is so great,
But think of each coin as a light in the darkness
And, joined together, puts food on a plate.

Sometimes we see evil, injustice and vice
And our hearts beat much faster, but what can we do?
We could wring our hands and say "That's so not nice"
Or join up with others you know will win through.

We all have potential to shine in the darkness,
If God lives inside us then we're full of light.
So think what you're doing and saying tomorrow
And shine in our world with the most brilliant light!

Cathedrale de St. Etienne, Metz.

Large and lofty, looming proudly over the city
St.Etienne beckons the faithful, the curious, the hopeful.
Dark and cool, see flickering candles, taking the prayers of the saints -
Of the hearts that are faint, of the faithful, of the hopeful.
Stained glass abounding – each and every window,
The older the paler, the newer the bright. rich reds, blues, greens, gold,
Showing the folk in the stories of old.
Pale faces of saints and peaky apostles – the style of craftsmen so long ago.
Sculptures so real that you just have to touch them,
The soft folds are hard, the lined skin so cold.
The neck-aching height of the vaulted roof above
Made with such skill, such sweat, such love.
Where is God in this grand masterpiece?
Are you there, Lord?

Step into sunshine that warms stones and skin.
Relieved of a burden? Of guilt? Of sin?
Past the two beggars, bent forward, ever hopeful.
Surely the pious can spare a few coins?
Is Jesus the carpenter standing there with them?
Uplifting the weary arms that hold the begging bowls?
The one who loves sinners and beggars and outcasts,
The unlovely and the unwashed.
The sun warms the skin but does the heart stay cold?
Are you there, Lord?

When evening falls and the mundane is done,
When the music's playing in the street cafes,
Loved ones hold hands and gaze into eyes – ever faithful?
Giggling girls eye the red-blooded Romeos – ever hopeful.
Are you there, Lord?

The curtains are drawn but, peeping out, one solitary traveller surveys the scene
– St. Etienne rising above the red rooftops, still faithfully inviting, still haughty,
Floodlit, for the tourist? In gold and aquamarine.
The emptying squares, the quietening streets,
The desperate addict, the gut-aching winos, the girls of the night – ever hopeful.
Are you there, Lord?

The stars are twinkling – ever faithful, the gentle breeze kisses the leafy trees.
"Yes, I'm there, and there, and there, and there – I'm faithful – for ever".

A Psalm of Praise

All of creation praises you, mighty God.
Everything radiates gladness in your presence.
The sun causes the earth to smile,
The moon creates wonder in our hearts.
The stars are a testimony to your power.
The clouds follow after you to the ends of the earth.
The stormy winds shout out your greatness.
The lightning crackles your majesty.
The summer breeze whispers your gentleness.
The ripples on the water tell where you've been.
The ripening buds call out your thoughtfulness.
The new leaves burst forth with joy.
The new-born lambs cannot be kept still.
All the baby creatures are full of your excitement.
The dormant bushes erupt with your colour.
The seasons roll on, telling of your faithfulness.
The tall trees clap their hands.
The tiny flowers nod their heads in agreement.
The rain clouds shower us with your blessings.
The snowflakes blanket us with your love.
The streams sing and laugh with your provision.
The waterfalls roar out your might.
The tall wheat and barley clothe their fields with your compassion.
Fruit and vegetables swell with pride as you fill them with goodness.
And man, made in your image, gives back to you
The praise and thankfulness that you have put in his heart.
All creation praises you, Creator and Sustainer.
Everything delights in your presence.

Autumn Leaves

They have to fall – don't fight it.
It's part of life – to die.
That leaf that was so fresh and green,
Full of hope and new life,
It burst forth – it danced – it waved.
It soaked up the sun –
It drank the rain –
It held on strong in the breeze and gales.

It spent its time – it lived,
It breathed and confidently shared in the life
Of the canopy.
It served its purpose – what was that?
God saw it – God birthed it – God used it.

Now the coolness turns it yellow,
Bronze or gold or red or brown.
Brittle and crisp – it's lost its charm –
Lost its strength and falls to earth.

It's gone but don't be sad,
You've done your bit – let it go.
Now the creatures will use it for food –
For bedding and a home.
Nature will use it for a mulch,
It's not been wasted.

Let it go – the season has passed.
Time to rest until the rising sap
Tells you it's time to prepare again –
Another task – another leaf – another walk of obedience.

Born Free

You began in my mind – I thought of you.
I fashioned you in my imagination and
I loved you before you were.
I gave your soul freedom.
Then I gave your soul a body –
A body to relate to other bodies
But your soul will be free.

Your body grew – your mind understood.
Your heart experienced –
Experienced life,
Experienced joy, love, pain, hurt.
Childish innocence learnt life.
Joy was tarnished – love was tainted.
You embraced life – but disappointments crowded in.

I held out my hands to you and for brief moments –
When you looked for those hands –
We danced together – free together.

Constraints surround you – hem you in,
But your soul is still free. Come and dance with me.
Life is holding you back but you can soar with me.

Close your eyes and look at me, what do you see?
I have no limits – you can melt into me
And your soul can soar with me, far away from life's constraints.

See, we're dancing together – your hands in mine,
High above the hurting and pain.
There's no fear with me. Can you feel my love?
Now do you understand total acceptance?
You were born of me.
You were meant to be.
Your shackles are of the world but your soul is never imprisoned.

Trust me with your soul.
Your soul is mine.
You are mine –
Wherever –
Always.

Father's Love (Based upon Psalm 139)

As I drove home today feeling so full of joy,
I realised I had this big grin on my face.
I was pondering on my childhood days,
and that even then life was full of your grace.

But then my thoughts went further back
to long before the day of my birth,
For even there, in my dear mother's womb,
I was woven together in the depths of the earth.

In that secret place you were forming me –
planning my life and ordaining my days,
My unformed body was not hidden from you –
oh how can I comprehend your ways?

All those years as my body grew
and my mind was filled with earthly things
You hemmed me in, behind and before,
and shielded me beneath your wings.

I made mistakes and went my own way
but you were there watching over me.
You knew my thoughts, and still you cared,
such knowledge is too wonderful for me!

Now I am grown and you have my heart,
I am yours for all eternity,
But still you want me to be as a child
and look upon you as a parent to me.

So, as I walk this earthly life,
when the pressure's on and I get in a muddle,
I lift my arms to my heavenly dad
and you pick me up and give me a cuddle.

Oh, I may stumble but I'll not fall
'cause I've felt you holding both my hands.
"Don't be anxious" you said "just trust in me
and I'll lead you to uncharted lands".

I don't have to try to be what I'm not,
you say you accept me, just as I am.
I can't earn your love, it's so freely given –
'twas at Calvary, sacrificing The Lamb.

How precious to me are your thoughts O God –
how vast! I can scarce understand
That were I to try to count them all
they would outnumber all the grains of sand.

To think that the God of the universe
created and cares for little ol' me.
From birth to death, before and beyond,
oh how can I *not* sing so thankfully!

Frustration of a Sinner

What are we but sinful wretches?
Full of ego, full of pride.
How can we be just like Christ was
when the gap it yawns so wide.

In the Bible there it tells us
of the graces we should know (Galatians 5: 22-23)
All essential if we are to have
a truly Christ-like glow.

The fruit of the Spirit is love for all man,
peace and patience, kindness too.
Easy enough for a short while each day,
but continuously not easy to do.

Goodness and faithfulness and humility,
all worldly things us should not please.
Add a measure of self-control,
there is no law against things as these.

When the Holy Spirit fills us
how we feel that we have changed!
Full of joy and full of love,
our whole being's rearranged!

How sure we are we'll do no wrong,
disciples now we aim to be.
With Christ beside us, how can we fail?
Only still waters we can see.

Then comes the day we see ourselves
with no more patience than the next,
See ourselves as Jesus sees us
it's no wonder we're perplexed.

It's like looking in a mirror
and not liking what we see.
Oh, too oft' we lose our tempers,
never knew how hard 'twould be.

All the vengeful thoughts we harbour,
fret and worry all the day.
Oh, how glad that Jesus promised
to take these awful sins away.

How hard it is to turn your cheek
when unkind words are spoken.
How hard to love your fellow man
when promises are broken.

What about our worldly treasures?
Not so easy to put aside.
We are meant to have no pleasures
unless Christ in them abides.

Nice to know that God is patient –
understands our lack of grace.
Enough to know that he will help
us if we pray and seek his face.

A Winter's Tale

Branches bare in winter's grip
But still reaching for the sky.
Pale sun highlighting every twig,
They seem to strain to reach on high.

The leaves have fallen long ago.
Brittle boughs brave the isolation,
But deep inside it's still alive
Just waiting for its transformation.

As we mature – our spring leaves gone
And winter's icy blasts are a trial,
We lay aside the striving world
And rest our weary limbs awhile.

Our spirits reach for the coming Son,
The freedom and the warmth He'll bring.
We'll be transformed and age no more
When face to face we'll meet our King.

Grace

When I am called to give and give 'til I am spent and worn,
I wonder how I can go on, I feel so ripped and torn.

I give of time, I give of love, I'm constantly attending.
Sometimes I'm just not sure it's me, but that I'm just pretending.

I tell myself I can't say NO, I'm really weak, not strong.
I seem to have no time for me. Are my priorities wrong?

Sometimes I think I've given too much, I'd dearly love to receive -
To be pampered and spoilt and have my own way, oh self-pity – you can deceive!

Then I read your holy word - how Jesus gave and gave,
He gave so much in those three years, and it didn't stop at the grave.

But you showed me there how it was done – Jesus also received,
But not from man who let him down – 'twas You to whom he cleaved!

He went alone and sought you out, he talked and listened and prayed.
'Twas there you filled him so full of you. He needed his Father's aid.

When he'd received and he was filled, down the mountain he came
And then he taught and raised the dead and healed the sick and lame.

You said to me "Come close, my child, I'll give you what men can't.
Receive from me and drink your fill, and what you need I'll grant."

"You give because I live in you but you can't give of your own.
It must be my love, my strength, my joy, – mine and mine alone"

"So, feast on me and be equipped for all I call you to do.
Don't strive, just trust, and rest in me, my grace is sufficient for you."

Hope For a Year

Those new year resolutions bring
A surge of hope to start the day,
But oh how soon the will power fades.
I know – let's book a holiday!
Now Spring is coming, and Easter time,
New buds are forming and lambs are born.
The cross brings hope of eternal life –
A thought to hold on to when we're forlorn.

Those Summer brides – the warmth of love,
Together forever they promise to stay.
For me, at last, that holiday's here,
Oh I do hope the sun comes out today.
The kids take exams they've got to pass
If Uni and a career's in their sights.
All their ambitions are pinned on that letter.
Is it joy or despair in those hot August nights?

Oh no! Is that Santa in the shops already?
But no job – and money for just one lottery ticket,
But look at the birds as they see Autumn berries
They haven't lost hope as they dive in the thicket.
There was talk of an Indian Summer this year
But the chill and the damp and the fog says "Not so!"
However, excitement and joy's in the air
And everyone's face has a real sort of glow!

Perhaps it's the parties, new love, or proposal,
Or the promise of presents now under the tree.
Anticipation of loved-ones' homecoming,
Everyone's living in this expectancy.
The gift of the Babe born in Bethlehem,
The promise of old brings us cheer,
So, we can find strength when the tinsel's all gone
To look forward to another new year.

Creation Around Us

My heart is bursting with thanks to you, Creator God,
For my eyes enjoy so much beauty around me.

You have created the azure sky, and velvety night with its millions of stars,
You have formed the wispy and billowing cloud formations.

You have made the tiny birds and filled them with sweet voices,
You have given us the animals to share our lives, our homes, our love.

You decided to let us see colour in the flowers, movement in the trees,
You chose texture for us to touch and water to slip through our fingers.

Your imagination is in the warmth and in the coolness,
Your mind is in the breeze and the stillness.

You are all around us.

Our eyes may grow dim and not see the beauty so clearly,
Our ears may not catch all the sounds around us,
Our voices may not be so tuneful or strong,
Our bodies may not be able to praise you so energetically,

But, you are still all around us.

Whether we have much or have little,
Whether we are strong or weak,
Whether all's well with the world or troubles and grief surround us,
Whether we are at peace or fighting our own little battles,

It's so good to know
You will always be
Around us.

Journeying Together

Come, follow me, let me lead you on a journey we can make together.
You won't leave the world behind but you'll take another path with me:
With me means I'll be with you.

I'll be in front showing the way but I'll be beside you
so you can hear what I say.
I'll be behind you so you need not fear.
Will you trust me? Will you give yourself to me?
Giving yourself means I'll give my all to you.

I won't always take you out of troubles
But we'll be in them together, you and me,
And I am in control of your troubles.
You will grow closer as you turn to me.
Turning to me means I can help you.

The world will still tempt you; The choice will still be yours;
But because you'll know that I am still with you
You'll hear my voice, your conscience, speaking clear.
Hearing my voice means strength for your will.

Some friends may mock and forsake you.
You'll not be the same person they knew.
Your values will change and you'll soften inside
But I will be your very best friend forever.
Being your best friend means I accept you just as you are.

A new love I will give you; You'll be surprised how you feel about others.
A heart full of joy will cause you to burst into song,
And a peace from deep within will overwhelm you.
Being overwhelmed means being full of my Spirit.

You may stumble, trip, or limp or fall, but I'll forgive and lift you up
And carry you 'til your strength returns
And we can walk hand in hand together again.
Hand in hand means I'm holding you and will never let you go.

Bring your baggage with you, your heavy load of shame,
Your suitcase of resentment that you hug to yourself.
As we walk, you'll cast them off one by one.
Our relationship brings lighter loads and empty bags.
Lighter loads means that I will have taken your heaviness,

Our path brings many crossroads and choices you'll have to make.
You'll say "I want my own way, But, which is Your way?"
Just listen and obey.
Obedience means choosing My Way, the right path,
the only path that will take you to the end of your journey.

Just Being – A Tree

You showed me the tree that's just there 'to be',
Doing nothing but growing; planted tenderly.
As branches grew bigger, some grew the wrong way;
The gardener has chopped them, the scar's there to stay.

But shoots have grown from them and given it form,
That's helped it to flourish and weather the storm.
Right now it looks bare but its shape has a grace
And new buds are forming as spring comes apace.

Leaves will soon adorn it and colour it green,
But what does it do? What does it mean?
Well, whether it's clothed or whether it's bare
It's home for the insects and birds of the air.

They need it, they use it, just 'cause it's a tree.
It doesn't do anything, it just has 'to be'.
People look at it, just passing at leisure;
Their eyes see its beauty. That tree gives them pleasure.

It gives us our oxygen – gives the world life!
Doesn't get worn out with stresses and strife.
The gardener is happy enjoying his tree
Seeing it 'do' just what it's meant 'to be'.

Just Being – Me

You want me 'to be' so that I can 'do'
And as long as I abide with you
You'll use what I am – what you helped me to be
To bring the praise and glory to thee.

You say "Be salt and bring out my taste –
Be used for preserving so none go to waste."
You say "Be light and shine out for me –
Be light in the darkness so sinners may see."

You say "Be perfume so people can smell
The fragrance of Jesus, and not go to hell."
Only one thing is needed, I'll choose what's best,
I only need strive to enter your rest.

It Is Finished

Lashing, scourging, stinging, smarting,
Flesh oozing red –
Blood spattering.
Cutting, slicing, painful, burning,
Flesh open to the bone –
Blood dripping.

Stumbling, lurching, staggering, falling
Under the weight
Of the wooden beam.
Reeling, light-headed through the crowd to Golgotha,
Thorny crown piercing –
Blood trickling.

Nails hammering, stabbing, fixing,
Lacerated back
Against splintery tree.
Lifting upwards, dropping, hanging.
Crowds mocking –
Mother's tears falling.

Sweating, gasping, "Father, forgive."
Spear thrusting -
Water gushing.
Heart heavy under the burden of the world's sin.
Head dropping –
Blood pouring –

"It is finished."

My Helper

You're a rock when my ground has crumbled,
A muscle when I feel weak.
You're an anchor when I think I'm drifting,
The sunshine when all seems bleak.

You're a breeze on my brow when I'm het up,
A cooling sponge when I fret.
You're an ice cube that melts my hot temper,
A tax rebate when I'm in debt.

You're a guide book when I'm feeling lost,
Prozak when I'm feeling pain.
You're a blanket when I'm needing a cuddle,
An umbrella when life starts to rain.

You're a taxi when I just can't go on,
A towel that absorbs all my tears.
You're a crane who raises my spirits,
A lion who carries my fears.

The Answer, My Friend.

How many times must I cry out for help
Before my Lord gets fed up with me?
And how many times do I say sorry again
Before I'm forgiven and free?

How many times will I covet and yearn
Before I'm content with what I've got?
And how many times do I do what I shouldn't
But don't do the good that I ought?

The answer, my friend, came like a gentle breeze,
"Remember the meaning of 'Grace'?
Don't be so hard on yourself, my child,
Perfection comes when you see me face to face."

Ode to a Stubborn One (from God)

You just don't know, my child, my son, how much I long for you
    To be a part of my family – yes, I want to adopt you too!

I want to be a father to you – even your mother if I may,
    To wrap my arms around you and wipe your tears away.

Oh, I know, you're a man, a macho guy, you don't need me at all.
Your stubbornness, your pride, your fears, deafens you to my call.

I make you uncomfortable don't I, son, I represent all that's weak,
    A figment of imagination at best, at worst – a "Jesus freak"!

You put on a show to cover your feelings, a laugh and a joke to hide
    Your doubts and insecurities, but I know what you're like inside.

I know what you're like but I love you still, I know what made you that way,
    For I knew you before you were born and I've loved you all the way.

I'd love you to come to me just as you are,
    don't worry I'm not asking you to pray
Or go to church to please your wife – I've got a much simpler way.

You know how often you think aloud – and talk to yourself a lot,
Well how about a debate with me about whether I exist - or not!

I'll let you be as rude as you like – sarcasm and anger I can take,
Put into words why you hate me so – just be honest for goodness sake.

Now be aware, I'm standing here – I'm really close to you
    So even if you just whisper to me, then I will talk to you too.

New Beginnings

It's dark and warm but very cramped and I'm all on my own.
I suck my thumb and turn around; this is my comfort zone.

Sometimes the noise is very loud, all gurgles, glugs and rumbles,
But I can hear a distant voice, of course it's mainly mumbles.

When my room is level and still and noises have subsided,
I think "I'll stretch a leg out now, which one I haven't decided."

But when my room turns on its side, I'm thrown all over the place.
I like it best being rocked to sleep on what's called 'Walking Pace'.

Hello – there's something going on, I'm getting squeezed all round.
My head is in a tunnel now and I hear a yelling sound.

I've never been this way before – head first towards some light,
But hey – there might be a bit more space although now it's very tight.

The yelling's getting louder, "Push hard" I think I hear.
Now suddenly it's very bright and someone's given a cheer!

Another yell – my arms are free, now my legs are everywhere!
Big hands are putting me on some scales and wiping my face and hair.

I'm wrapped up cosy and placed somewhere soft. I open my eyes to see
Two beaming faces so full of love that only have eyes for me.

I think I'm going to like these two, I've decided I shall linger.
I don't think it will be so very hard to wrap them round my little finger!

The Artist

With paintbrush in hand he looked at the globe.
He knew what he wanted to make.
He balanced his palette and dabbed with his brush –
There's no chance he'll make a mistake.

He mixed several blues and painted the sea,
Then brown merged with grey for the land.
Thick lumps topped with white took the flatness away;
Made thin strips of ochre for sand.

A lake here and there, a river or two,
Now that's all the water complete.
Next, he's blended some greens for the forests and grass;
Perhaps delicate leaves would look sweet.

A riot of orange and purple and pink,
And shades of red mixed together.
He dotted and dabbed to colour the fruit,
The flowers, the gorse and the heather.

He put down his brush and picked up some clay
And softened it in his hand.
He fashioned it into the beasts and the birds –
'Twas just as he had planned.

"I'll make some people to tend the land,"
The artist thought with glee.
He shaped and smoothed and coloured their skin –
There was such variety.

At last, he stood and surveyed his work
But something was very odd.
There was no life – and he suddenly knew
He was only an artist – not God!

The River of Life

Dark and brooding
The current pushes relentlessly against me.
I swim against the flow – how tiring it is.
Strength is ebbing
But a boulder appears before me
And I clamber upon it gasping with relief.

The water sparkles as it rushes past me,
How easy it would be to slide in
Go with the flow, to be taken along –
Many others are laughing as they go past
But I know where they are heading,
I've seen the map.

Strengthened, I dive in,
Reinvigorated, full of hope.
Debris suddenly comes upon me,
Bruised I push it out of the way.
Swim on, swim on. Is this how a salmon feels?
Weeds are tangling around my legs,
They're trying to pull me under.

Why is this happening? I struggle to swim,
Struggle to breathe, struggle to free myself,
Then, my feet touch solid ground and I haul myself ashore.
I rest, drink from a pool of pure water
And sleep in safety.

Voices are calling me. "Keep going – we're with you".
I'm not alone. A hand reaches out towards me.
Refreshed yet again I plunge in.
"Stay with us – there's strength in numbers!"

Encouraged, I swim on,
Knowing there are plenty of rocks to rest upon.
Yes, I'll tire but I'll not give in.
Weeds, debris, logs, rapids – I *will* overcome,
Boulders, rocks, sandy beaches – I *will* gain strength.

Swim on, swim on
To the source – *there* I'll find rest for evermore.

Thoughts of Mary

Blessed among women! Yet what did you feel?
What thoughts filtered through your mind?
From the day when the angel o'er shadowed you
'Til the day your son died for mankind?
I have no knowledge of your childhood and youth,
But a nice child you must've been,
For you found great favour with Almighty God.
He knew just what it would mean.
Betrothed to Joseph, respected and liked,
Your future, you thought, was all clear,
But Almighty God had other plans for you
And he began by saying "Don't fear!"
The words of the angel did puzzle you
When told you would bear a son.
"How will this be, for I've known no man?"
But the work of the Lord had begun.
I've read that you were willing to be
The mother of the Son of Man,
But I wonder if you had doubts and fears
As the angel unfolded God's plan?
"What will my friends say? What will Joseph do?
Imagine the Lord choosing me!
My son is going to reign forever!
The Son of God! Can it really be?"
You shared your joy with Elizabeth,
Oh how happy you must've both been,
Talking about the expected babes,
And all you had heard and seen.
And what about that Bethlehem trip
On the back of a donkey no less!

A very heavily pregnant girl,
How did you cope with the stress?
The inn was full, no place to rest,
People were everywhere,
And when you started your labour pains
I wonder – what was your prayer?
The only place to bear your child
Was dirty, crude and lowly.
Did you wonder if God had made a mistake
With the birthplace of one so Holy?

No mother or best friend there to help you,
No friends outside a-waiting,
Just Joseph and the animals.
What *was* God demonstrating?
The child was born and wrapped in cloths,
No fancy layette and shawl.
No cosy cradle with blue lace trim.
Just straw – in a cattle stall!
Then the shepherds came to visit you
And what wondrous stories they brought!
They knew that your son was Christ, the Lord,
That he was the One they sought.
"The glory of the Lord shone around us" they said,
"And an angel told us of you,
Then a whole host of angels appeared and sang,
And praised God through and through."
Well Mary, you treasured up all these things
And pondered them in your heart.
You hadn't been alone had you?

And this was just the start!
The angels were celebrating in heaven,
The Saviour's here at last!
Oh Mary, the Christ is *your* little boy!
Your heart must've beat so fast.
You didn't know then what was to come,
When Jesus became a man.
You couldn't guess about the humble life,
And the miracle of God's plan.
There was no room for Jesus at the inn that day,
And years later – no room in men's hearts.
You couldn't foresee the Lord on the cross
And the cloud on which he departs.
But Mary, your little babe changed the world!
He saves us from our sin
When we say "Yes, dear Lord, there's room
In MY heart, come on in!"

Though Mountains May Fall Into The Sea

You are anxious about so many things
From minor ailments to nuclear war,
Yet your fears are all important to me,
You see, I know why you fear.

I see what surrounds you, what you might miss
If it were all taken away.
I know what could happen to you
If you lost your security.

There are so many things that could all go wrong,
Be it health or home or family;
A fire, a flood, a hurricane, war,
A terminal illness or just old age.

But what is the worst thing? To face alone your trials?
Or the final moment of death?
Well, either of these – you'll find me there –
With you in your pain and fear.

When you go through that final door my hand will be in yours,
My arms will lift you into my very presence.
You will see me face to face – you are mine.
So do not be anxious, still your fearful heart and know that I am God.

I am your refuge –
This very moment –
And for ever.

Come Unto Me My Child *(Song)*

Come unto me my child,
Pour out your troubled mind,
Tell me all that worries you,
Your fears of every kind.

Chorus
For I will uplift you
And I'll give you rest.
I'll comfort and hold you
And give you what's best.
Just take on my yoke
That's easy and light.
I'll love and protect you
And do what is right.

Come unto me my child,
Give me your hurting heart.
Lay it down before me
The pain will then depart.

Chorus

Come unto me my child
Those burdens weigh too much.
Leave them all beside me,
Accept my healing touch.

Chorus

Glory to God *(Song)*

Jesus says if we live in him
We will be like fruitful branches
And bring glory to God
Glory to God
Glory to God on high.

Jesus says if we do his commands
He will grant anything that we ask him
And bring glory to God
Glory to God
Glory to God on high.

Jesus says that as his true disciples
We'll produce abundant harvests
And bring glory to God
Glory to God
Glory to God on high.

Hallelujah Jesus is Risen!

Hallelujah Jesus is risen!
Hallelujah Christ's alive!
Judas had sold him
But the grave couldn't hold him
Hallelujah Christ's alive!

Hallelujah the Spirit is given!
Hallelujah he's everywhere!
Empowering, enlivening,
Heartening, inspiring,
Hallelujah Christ is here!

Hallelujah God is speaking!
Hallelujah He's moving now!
Prophetic words are given
Along with dreams and visions,
Hallelujah God is moving now!

God Loves Me! *(Song)*

I did not know – but now I know
How much I grieved the Lord.
How all my sin offended him
Why all his blood out poured.
But now I know – yes now I know
God loves me!

I did not see – but now I see
Why Jesus had to die.
He took the place of my disgrace
And then he rose on high.
So now I see – yes now I see
God loves me!

I did not feel – but now I feel
So grateful to my Lord.
He lives within – I'm dead to sin,
I'm set free by his word.
So now I feel – yes now I feel
God loves me!

I was not sure – but now I'm sure
Almighty God does care.
So quietly he speaks to me
And says he's always there.
So now I'm sure – yes now I'm sure
God loves me!

In the Beginning *(Song)*

In the beginning was God
And the Word reigned in heaven with him,
But the devil was greedy
So proud and so vain,
That sin entered the world
And brought heartache and pain
And this beautiful planet was spoiled.

Jesus was hated and spat on
By all those who thought they were so good,
But the humble and contrite
The lowly and meek
And the ones who were helpless
Who knew they were weak
Were forgiven, delivered and healed.

Judged and convicted and sentenced
By the crowd who were shouting for blood,
He was taken and beaten
And nailed to a tree,
There he died, crucified,
On his lips was the plea…
"Oh my Father, forgive them their sin."

Raised from the grave, he returned
Full of life, to the ones that he loved,
But when he had to leave them
He promised to send
A Help and a Comforter,
Guide and a Friend,
And so now Holy Spirit is here.

It's You and Me Jesus *(Song)*

No longer a slave but your friend Lord,
Sharing what God shared with you.
Telling me things that I need to know,
Revealing the truth so that I can grow,
Showing the next step that I should go,
It's you and me Jesus.

You never grow weary of listening Lord
To all my tales of woe.
Pouring out worries of every kind
I hand them to you and delight to find
You really do give me peace of mind,
It's you and me Jesus.

When out in this world full of strife Lord,
Surrounded by hatred and greed,
Hearing them take your name in vain
It bruises my soul and I feel your pain,
But you're there to comfort again and again,
It's you and me Jesus.

Together we face the day Lord,
You know just what it will bring.
I need not fear 'cause I trust you Lord,
I can face the enemy with your sword,
I could sail the world with you aboard,
It's you and me Jesus.

I'm never alone in the crowd Lord,
You're with me wherever I go.
Holding my hand you walk with me,
Taking my fears you set me free,
My heart's as light as it could be,
It's you and me Jesus.

Father in Heaven *(Song)*

Oh Father in Heaven how sad you must be
When you look at this world that you made perfectly.
There's so much that's wrong we can scarce take it in
So we beg you dear Father – forgive us our sin.

Chorus
Holy Spirit please help us to pray
As we come to your great throne of grace.
Speak to our heart,
Show us our part
As we come here to seek your sweet face.

Oh Jesus we feel your abhorrence of greed,
Some people are rich but so many in need.
Corruption and evil are festering within
So we beg you dear Jesus – forgive us our sin.

Chorus

Oh Lord we are feeling a burden so great.
You gave all that you had for a world full of hate.
Your love we should share but we keep it held in
So we beg you dear Lord – forgive us our sin.

Chorus

Will You Follow Me? *(Song)*

I whisper to you in the quietness,
My love I am longing to share.
Do you not feel my breath and my gentleness
As I tenderly show you I care?

Chorus
For I am calling you,
Oh will you follow me
And go where I want you to go?
Yes I'm inviting you
But will you follow me
Or will you turn away and say no?

I show you my blood shed at Calvary,
The tears and the pain I went through.
Do you not understand what I'm saying?
Oh my child I did all that for you.

Chorus

I've helped you when you prayed despondently,
I've always been there at your side,
But now I want you to respond to me
And come to my arms open wide.

Chorus

I've done all I can for your happiness,
I offer this gift to you free.
I just want to deal with your emptiness
And give you a life filled with me.

Chorus

Close Your Eyes *(Song)*

Close your eyes and feel his presence
Know the Lord is here.
'Tis he who loves you, won't you trust him?
Give him all your fear.
As he puts his arms around you
And you feel his warmth surround you
Give up all those heavy burdens,
Wipe away your tear.

Savour now that blessed stillness
Of a peaceful heart.
He's put joy so deep within you
Feel a smile start.
As you realise his power
And with blessings he will shower,
Know that he's your mighty refuge
From the fiery dart.

Feel the praise well up inside you
To your heart above.
Let your spirit rise unhindered
Soaring like a dove.
As you see him smile with pleasure
And you know that you're his treasure
You'll go on to live in victory
Strengthened by his love.

We Praise and we Worship you Lord *(Song)*

We praise and we worship you Lord
Our Saviour and Heavenly King
For you indeed are worthy
Of all the praise we could bring.
Worthy to be exalted, Lord over everything.

We lift up the name of Jesus,
Redeemer and Holy One.
You shall receive the glory
That's due to God's only Son.
Honour and praises for all that you have done.

Almighty God and Creator,
Such gentle love you impart.
So mighty yet caring
Causing our fear to depart.
Praise and thanksgiving come from our grateful hearts.

Ring Out Those Bells *(Song)*

Ring out those bells – and sing our Saviour's praises.
The Lord has come – to save our dying world.
Left behind his majesty
Born a helpless baby,
That glorious day – salvation was unfurled.

Ring out those bells – let's celebrate this Christmas.
O joyous time – when Jesus Christ was born.
Shepherds came and angels sang,
Wise men came from far-off lands.
He is the Christ – O happy happy morn.

Ring out those bells – and tell the world of Jesus.
All Christians sing – let's join the happy throng.
He changed the course of history,
O what a marvellous mystery,
We'll praise his name – and sing this Christmas song.

Introduction to Letters

In writing these letters, I have sought to understand how sometimes obscure characters in Bible stories saw things and I have written it in a way to appeal to all ages.

Between September 2014 and July 2019 I volunteered at 'The Word' – an after school Bible class run by Woodard Chaplain Paul Sanderson. Paul and two lads – Judah and Taz – turned five of the letters into You Tube videos, hopefully supporting charity Links International.[1]

Forgive me when I have added a word or name such as Pheobe in 'The Elated Father', as Jairus's daughter was not named as far as I know. Obviously, some of the relative's or friend's names are fictional.

I pray that you will find something in each page that opens up a familiar Bible story and speaks to you or your circumstances.

---

1 youtube.com: The Word – The Bible a Different Way - Pauline's Postings Ep 1 to 6

Letter from a Big Sister
(Moses in the Bullrushes)

Greetings to my Dearest Friend Rachel,

Sorry we haven't been able to meet up for a long time but any message I send could get us into trouble. However, this postman is a good reliable friend of Dad's.

Remember when Pharaoh ordered that every newborn Hebrew boy must be killed because there are so many of us? Well Mum and Dad went and had another baby but managed to hide him for three months until he was about to be discovered. What a dilemma! We were so scared. Well Mum had made a tiny but sturdy basket out of papyrus reeds and waterproofed it with tar and pitch, so she put my baby brother in it and we went down to the river where lots of tall reeds grew. I stayed with him for a while until some Egyptian ladies came along so I hid and watched. I'm not sure if Mum was going to pop back and feed him every few hours or if she knew Pharaoh's daughter bathed there but suddenly this beautiful lady spotted the basket in the reeds, sent her slave girl to get it and I thought "I've blown it now – we've lost him. Am I in trouble or what!"

However, when she opened the basket, my little brother started crying – maybe all her eye make-up scared him – Mum didn't look like that! She recognised him as one of the Hebrew babies but instead of handing him over to be killed she was speaking as if she wanted to keep him and raise him herself! As her son and heir no less!

Well, Rachel, without even thinking too hard about it, I jumped out of hiding. Actually I think God might have pushed me from behind. I asked if she'd like me to find a nursing woman who could feed him. She cuddled him a bit and I could see she didn't want to hand him over but realised she couldn't nurse him herself so she told me to find someone and she would pay. Mum couldn't believe that she had her son back and we were a family again – for a while.

Every so often Mum took my baby brother to see the Pharaoh's daughter by the river and we could all see the woman really loved him. Well we knew that when he was weaned he would have to go and we all cried a lot when the time came. However, Mum and Dad reckoned that God had a plan for the boy, that maybe he was special and needed to learn languages and skills and authority, so their grief was tinged with hope. Pharaoh's daughter named him Moses, which means 'draw out' as she had taken him out of the water.

We miss him terribly Rachel but he's in God's hands and, I think, in God's plans.

Maybe we could meet up again soon, Rachel,

From your friend Miriam

Exodus 2

Letter from Cleopas
(Road to Emmaus)

Greetings Samuel,

When we last met together we were discussing the fact that I was a follower of the Rabbi Jesus and you were anticipating a crisis. Well, you no doubt heard that the crisis ended with the trial and crucifixion of our dear Jesus which devastated us all.

Well my friend, something amazing happened to me after that which you may not have heard about.

My friend and I had left the believers in Jerusalem and were returning broken-hearted, totally disillusioned and disappointed to Emmaus when a stranger joined us on the road who seemed to be the only person who didn't know what had happened. We told him how we were expecting Jesus to rescue the nation of Israel from its Roman rulers and said that even after he had been killed his body had disappeared from the tomb despite being closely guarded. Some women said that they had seen him since but we didn't believe them.

This stranger said we were foolish then started to explain the Scriptures from Moses and the Prophets which had foretold all this. We were riveted so when we reached our village we asked him to stay over and while we were eating he broke the bread and suddenly we recognised that he was our Jesus – we had been so absorbed in our own grief and disappointment we couldn't see beyond our noses. We knew that he was explaining the Scriptures but now it all fell into place that he was the promised Messiah but it was we who had misunderstood his purpose. Suddenly however, Jesus disappeared and we looked at one another with our mouths open and a look of joyful amazement on our faces.

Well I don't know what the time was but we jumped up and made our way back to Jerusalem where we found the other disciples who were also jumping for joy so we told them our story.

Oh Sam, you may not believe this bit but, here goes; Jesus actually appeared in the room among us and as we were all in a state of shock he showed us his hands and feet where he had been nailed to the cross and invited us to touch him!!! He then ate a piece of fish – just to prove a point! Well all this changed us from downcast and disillusioned to faith-filled and on-fire but, d'you know Sam, I'm sure this is the just the beginning of something HUGE and exciting so, come and join me so you can be part of it. You won't regret it.

See you soon, Cleopas

Luke 24: 13-49

Letter from a Cross-carrier
(Simon of Cyrene)

To my dearest sister Kiria,

Just to let you know that I am staying in Jerusalem a bit longer than I expected as events happening here are life-changing!

My journey from Cyrene was long and tiring but I'd only just got into Jerusalem for the Passover celebrations when I saw three men being led out of the city carrying large wooden crosses on their backs. As they approached, one of the men collapsed in front of me – he had been flogged so was very bloody and weak. Suddenly a guard grabbed me and forced me to pick up the cross of the man Jesus. People had been telling me about the amazing miracles he had done and the way he had spoken with authority, claiming he was the Messiah so I was very shocked that it was me helping him.

Jesus staggered ahead of me so I could see the people in the crowd and how they reacted to him. Some were shouting out insults but others, especially the women, were crying fit to burst. They must have been close friends and family because he managed to turn and speak to them briefly.

Well we all stumbled out of the city to a hill where, apparently, the Romans executed criminals publicly as an example to others. I was glad to hand over the cross and melt away into the crowd where I watched as the three men were nailed to their crosses and left hanging there to die. It was so awful Kiria, watching his family sobbing away as he grew weaker. I think I'll have nightmares about it for ever.

After a while I went to find my lodgings but at some point the whole place shook and went dark and I know now that was when Jesus died.

A few days later there were rumours going around that Jesus' body had disappeared and, amazingly, people had seen him alive, so I'm going to hang around Jerusalem a bit longer as I feel as if something momentous is happening here and I want to be in on it! Seems like his claims were true and I want to find out more about him.

See you when I get home, Sis,

Love Simon

Luke 23 v26

Letter from a Damp Disciple
(Jesus Walks on Water)

To Aaron, my dear friend, and greetings to you and your dear wife, Suzanna.

Thank you for your kind invitation to kip at yours when I'm next in your locality, it will be a pleasure, especially to give you the latest gen on all that my Teacher, Jesus, is up to. But I can't wait to tell you about some amazing things which happened recently.

Only the other day I watched him miraculously feed thousands of people who had come to listen to his teachings but what happened later really blew my mind and has given me such faith to believe in him. After such a long, hot time teaching, he said he wanted to be alone to talk to God, to sort of re-charge his batteries I suppose so he told us to get into the boat, cross the Sea of Galilee and he would see us later, and off he went, alone.

Well I must have slept in the boat for a few hours but the sudden storm woke me up and, good heavens, were those waves big – and I'm used to the squalls on this lake. I have to admit I was afraid we'd had it – clinging on for dear life, bailing out water and not seeing any sign of the far bank even though the moon kept peeping out of the clouds.

It was on one of those 'moon-peeps' that we saw Jesus – yes, in the middle of the lake, in the middle of the night, there he was, walking towards us, on the water! Well, we all thought he was a ghost at first until he spoke to us above the noise of the waves and told us not to be afraid. I don't know if I was shivering with cold and wet or dreadful fear but it was funny how that word from Jesus calmed my soul.

Anyway, rash, impulsive, impetuous Peter shouted out, "Master, if it's really you, call me to come out to you on the water." Whaaat?

"Come on then" Jesus answered him, so Peter got out and actually started walking on the water towards Jesus! How brave! What faith!

Unfortunately he looked down at the water churning under and around him, started to sink and cried out to Jesus to save him, which of course he did – just reached out and grabbed him and the two of them clambered into the boat. Then the waves calmed down and we were all awestruck by the power that Jesus had and we all realised that he truly was God's Son, for sure! I'm still blown away by Jesus' knowing where we were and what was happening – was he watching us from the mountain and how did he get to us so quickly? Gosh, in trouble? – call for Jesus!

When we reached the shore word got around and, again, crowds gathered, bringing the sick with them and all who touched his coat were healed. Then he started teaching again – all in a day's work for Jesus even though he'd had no sleep. What a man! I hope that's whetted your appetite to hear more of his amazing exploits when I get to you.

Peace be with you all.

James

Matthew 14: 22-33

Letter from David's Servant
(David and Abigail)

Greetings Cousin Baruch,

We haven't met up for quite a while as I'm on the run with my master, David, but I am so bursting to tell you about recent events in my life I thought I'd get a message to you.

As I said, my master, David is trying to keep out of the way of King Saul and we had got to the Desert of Maon where a rich man called Nabal was shearing his many thousands of sheep (well, his men were). David sent ten of us to greet Nabal and politely ask if we could have whatever he could spare as we had protected his herds at Carmel.

However, Nabal's reply was a tad rude, especially as our culture is to be hospitable and generous and he was wealthy enough to spare some sheep and goats – well, enough for about 600 men. So we reported back to David who flew off the handle and got us all ready for a showdown with Nabal. Phew, was the air blue or what!

However, as we entered a mountain ravine we came across this beautiful woman who fell at David's feet and begged him to listen to her. She was Nabal's wife, Abigail and she apologised for her foolish husband and begged David not to be rash and take revenge out of anger because he would have it on his conscience that the Lord his God had not ordered it.

David calmed down immediately as he realised what he was about to do – though it might have been something to do with this gorgeous woman fluttering her lashes at him. She then showed him the gifts of food she had brought with her – my goodness, what a feast – bread, wine, mutton, roasted grain and hundreds of raisin cakes and fig cakes – all loaded on to donkeys ready for us to take back to camp.

David was impressed. Abigail went home to her husband.

Well, part two of the story is that, apparently, as Nabal was drunk when Abigail got home, she waited until he was sober in the morning – very wise – and told him what had happened. I can just imagine he would have gone purple with rage and probably tried to clobber her but, according to Abigail's maids, Nabal had a heart attack and ten days later, died!

David was so pleased that he hadn't killed him – ("Serve him right" I think I heard him say) and the next thing was

I was sent to go and fetch her to be David's wife!

This Abigail is quite a remarkable woman, Baruch, with wisdom and skills as well as beauty – Nabal didn't deserve her.

I'll tell you more if and when I get to visit you.

Give my regards to your wife,

Your cousin,

Kileab.

1 Samuel 25

Letter From a Doubter
(Noah's Ark)

My Dear Brother Amram,

I am sending this message to share with you my dilemma in the hope that we can decide together what we should do.

A man named Noah, living in my village, believes he has been told by God that a disastrous flood is coming upon us all because of our corrupt, violent and wicked ways. He has been told to build a HUGE boat for his family and he believes God will send pairs of every kind of living creatures to it to be saved.

I know you and I try to be good people but God hasn't spoken to me and I don't know whether to believe that Noah's heard the truth or is just scaremongering or is actually going mad. I mean, the river is a long way off and the mist is a bit thick occasionally but, wipe us all out? It's a bit OTT isn't it?

If it's really true we ought to be helping Noah build his boat and earn our place on it when the time comes, after all he only has his family helping and it's a really big boat. But all our neighbours are taking the mickey out of him and abusing his family and I don't want that for me or mine.

Do you think we should buy up some provisions and go and make a new home up on the mountain? Hedge our bets so to speak?

We have to make a decision by the time his boat is ready but that could be months or years, and then what if a flood doesn't come? We'd be stuck on his boat with all those smelly, dangerous animals, birds and bugs, for who knows how long? We'd have put all our eggs in one basket, so to speak, lost our homes and reputations, for what?

Does God ever speak to you Amram? Sometimes I have thoughts and feelings, sometimes strange images and words in my mind but I've never discussed them with anyone for fear of looking and sounding stupid or mad. I wonder if it was God trying to tell me something?

Shall we meet up soon and you can tell me what you think – better not leave it too long, just in case…

Regards to your family,

Joash.

Genesis 6

Letter from an Elated Father
(Healing of Jairus' Daughter)

Greetings to my dear brother Reuben,

I had to write to you to tell you what just happened to my dear little girl. You may have had a message saying that she was dying but this letter is to tell you that she is now alive and well! And all because of the itinerant rabbi, Jesus.

I had intended to hear this Jesus speak because, as you know, as synagogue ruler it's my job to find a rabbi to preach on the Sabbath. However, my thoughts that day were all about young Phoebe so when I heard Jesus was in town I rushed out, shoved my way through the crowds and fell at his feet, pleading with him to come and lay his hands on Phoebe and heal her.

Jesus helped me up and we started for home but we were delayed by some poor, sick woman who had touched his cloak and received instant healing. Despite my urgent needs Jesus made time for her and was so compassionate.

However, just then my friends came and told me Phoebe had died and not to bother Jesus any more – we were too late! Just as I was about to turn into a blubbering wreck Jesus said to me "Don't be afraid, just believe and she will be healed."

That gave me a shred of hope so I led Jesus and a few of his followers to my house where there was the customary weeping and wailing from the crowd of mourners. Jesus asked them why they were wailing – she wasn't dead, just asleep!

Well Reuben, one doesn't make a mistake like that very easily so they laughed at him. I realised afterwards that he meant she was only temporarily dead. Jesus tolerated the crowd because he wanted them to realise that faith in him brings about the impossible.

Well, the wife and I, plus Jesus and his friends went in Phoebe's bedroom and there Jesus gently took her by the hand and just said "Little girl, get up". And, Reuben – she did!

He told the wife, who was nearly screaming with joy, to give her some food and told us not to spread the news – as if we could keep quiet! But I knew if everybody got to hear they would only want miracles from him when he wanted them to listen to his words that would heal their broken spiritual lives.

And you should have heard his words in our synagogue that Sabbath – they were electrifying! I will tell you more about this amazing man, what he says and who he really is but that's for when I see you next.

Blessings on you brother,

Jairus.

Matthew 9: 18, Mark 5: 21 and Luke 8: 40

Letter From Elisha's Servant
(Chariots of Fire)

Hi Dad,

Sorry I haven't been in touch lately but I hope this news makes up for it.

As I am Elisha's servant (and I like to think, his friend) I get to see some awesome things that our God does and, recently, I saw the most awesome thing in my life (even compared to Elisha raising people from the dead!) God had told Elisha where the Aramean army was going to be so he was able to warn the king of Israel, who believed Elisha's words every time.

The king of Aram was furious with Elisha and, unbeknown to us, sent loads of men out to Dothon to capture him.

Well, I got up early the next morning to discover the army with horses and chariots had surrounded the city. I was really scared and thought it would be the end for us but, upon asking Elisha what we should do, he just seemed really calm and told me,

"Don't be afraid, those who are with us are more than those who are with them."

Huh! I'm no good at sums but even I could see that us two against an army doesn't add up.

Elisha asked God to open my eyes so that I might see! Surely he could see that my eyes were open and out on stilts!

However, and I don't blame you if you don't believe this, Dad, but suddenly I saw that the hills were full of horses and chariots OF FIRE all around us. I realised that I was actually seeing God's heavenly army and all my fears evaporated (I think I let out a whoop of excitement!)

Then, as the enemy came towards us, Elisha asked God to strike them all blind – and God did just that!

Floundering in their blindness, they didn't know that it was Elisha, the man they were looking for, who came up to them and told them to follow him.

So, Elisha led them into the city of Samaria, then asked God to open their eyes again – which He did! The look of surprise on their faces made me hoot with laughter until I realised that the king of Israel was about to kill them. However, the king asked the advice of Elisha who said he was not to kill them and he wasn't to take the credit for what God had done.

So he fed and watered them and sent them back to Aram. I think I've heard of a proverb that says something about "heaping burning coals upon their heads." Anyway we haven't had any more trouble from them.

So remember, Dad, if ever you're afraid, call upon God who has more resources than you could dream of.

All God's blessings to you and Mum.

Gehazi

2 Kings 6: 8-23, Proverbs 25: 21-22

Letter From a Foolish Young Lady
(The Coming Bridegroom)

Dearest Sapphira,

I'm telling you what's just happened to me so that hopefully, it won't happen to you.

You see, my friends and I were going to join in a wedding procession and go to the reception at the bridegroom's house. We'd all been invited even though some of us didn't know him, so us ten girls got all dressed up and went out to wait for him to come along.

We didn't know how long he'd be, so as it was getting near dusk we took our torches and sat down to wait. Well the hours went by and we all dozed off until suddenly someone called out,

"The bridegroom's here! Come and greet him!"

Of course it's midnight, pitch black, can't see a thing, so we all turned our torches on only for some to find out the batteries were dead!

Now, five girls had thought ahead and had been prepared with spare batteries, so they went off leaving us five calling after them, but they had none to spare so we groped our way back to town to try to buy some more – as if any of our shops would be open 24/7. So we went to all our neighbours begging and borrowing some batteries, then went to find the bridegroom's house.

Unfortunately we were too late – the doors were locked and we weren't allowed in. We called out to the bridegroom but he said,

"I'm sorry, I don't know you" and I'm sure he had tears in his eyes.

I was absolutely gutted that I was left outside, especially as some friends had tried to tell me to be well prepared, and I hadn't listened.

So, Saffy, if you've had an invitation, don't take it for granted, like me. Get to know Jesus, the bridegroom. Be prepared because you can't rely on anyone else's batteries and because you just don't know the exact hour that he's coming.

Lots of love from your friend

Zillah

Matthew 25

Letter from a Happy Girl
(Jesus Rides into Jerusalem)

Greetings Cousin Rachel,

I've just been out with the crowds in Jerusalem and it's been awesome!

Remember when you told me about the man Jesus who'd been doing miracles and other amazing stuff? Well, he's just come to town and the crowds have gone wild!

As soon as I heard he was coming I joined the others cutting down branches and leaves to give him a right royal welcome, after all, people were saying he was going to be our king and save us all and that it was all foretold by our old prophets Isaiah and Zechariah.

Well, we rolled the red carpet out alright – some spreading out their coats as well and we were shouting out "Hosanna! Save us! Blessed is he who comes in God's name!"

But, d'you know, he wasn't all dressed up and on a big horse like I'd expected from a conquering hero or a king, he was dressed simply and riding on a donkey! Meekness not majesty.

Most of the crowd were full of hope and joy but I spotted some Pharisees watching it all and their faces seemed to show anger, envy? And even fear. I guess they thought their sanctimonious noses might be put out of joint. Ha ha, I do hope so.

Later on I heard that he's really upset them by turning over the money changers' tables in the temple so I'll find out more about this and let you know.

He does sound like a lovely king, Rachel, he seems to care for us ordinary folk and the downtrodden and children, even women!

Will write again after Passover. I have a feeling I may have more news for you then.

Say hello to your family for me,

Suzanna

Matthew 21: 1-11, Luke 19: 28-38

Letter from a Delighted Onlooker
(Turning Tables Over)

Greetings to my old friend Thomas,

In your last letter you asked whether I had any news of the rabbi Jesus who is claiming to be our Messiah, well I've just witnessed something quite remarkable so am writing while it's fresh in my mind.

Jesus of Nazareth really seems to stir things up wherever he goes and today he went to the temple area and caused uproar!

I had come to the temple to worship God and had brought one of my little lambs to sacrifice but was told it had a mark on it and wasn't perfect enough so I had to buy one from the merchants instead, at an awfully high price. Well, as you know, the merchants only accept the temple coins so I had to go to the kiosk of a money changer first – what a rigmarole. I didn't know the exchange rate so didn't seem to get much for my money – what a rip-off!

Anyway, next thing I knew Jesus and his followers came along. He stopped, looked around at what was going on, seemed to get very angry, then – oh my goodness, he really kicked off!

He overturned the tables with all their neat rows of coins, scattering them everywhere. He went from one to the other – people, tables, chairs, small animals and doves went flying. Firstly people were shocked but we all heard him say the temple was supposed to be a house of prayer but they were making it a den of robbers!

What a shambles – stallholders were trying to catch their animals and birds, beggars and children were scrabbling around on the floor picking up coins and the temple guards were trying to bring some sort of order but were overwhelmed by such a big crowd.

After the initial shock, I found myself cheering Jesus on. He saw the commercialism and injustice but actually did something about it. What a rebel! What an activist!

He was awesome, Thomas. A leader worth following I think. He was surrounded by people and children even, for hours, healing the blind and crippled and talking about his future kingdom. I'm going to get to know him better and find out about his kingdom, sounds an exciting place to be.

Will write again soon. Regards to your wife,

Benjamin.

Matthew 21: 12, Mark 11: 15-17

Letter From a Judgemental Man
(Woman Caught in Adultery)

Dearest Brother,

Thought I'd send you another message about the man, Jesus of Nazareth, who keeps making me think a lot about our religion and traditions.

The latest jolt was just now when I joined the other Pharisees in dragging an adulterous woman in front of him. I know we should have brought her lover out too but we were only doing it to trap Jesus into violating Moses' law.

We wanted to see if he would stop us stoning her (the legal penalty) but he did a very bizarre thing – he bent down and started writing on the ground with his finger!

We kept badgering him until he stood up and said "If any one of you is without sin, let him be the first to throw a stone at her", then he bent down again. What? Where did that bit of wisdom come from? Wow that made us think because we all knew deep down that none of us are sinless. And what was he writing down there? A list of our sins? The ten commandments? Or just a doodle?

The silence was deafening!

Well we all dropped our stones and slunk away but I stayed near enough to hear what he said to the woman.

Jesus stood up and asked her where everyone was and had no-one condemned her? She replied "No-one, Master" and he said "Nor do I condemn you but go and don't sin any more".

It made me think all the way home – he didn't ignore her sin nor condone it, he just showed compassion on her.

I guess when we see people doing wrong we just want to show our righteousness and come down on them like a ton of bricks – maybe we need to see ourselves as sinners more and be compassionate like Jesus. I like him and his wise words even though they make me squirm.

I'm sure I'll be writing again soon, Brother, as he stirs us up quite a lot.

God be with you,

Balphus

John 8: 1-11

Letter from a Kidnapped Little Girl
(Naaman's Healing)

Hi Mama,

Hope you get this note OK, it's been a while since I was taken from you in Israel by the raiders here in Aram in the north.

Well I work for a lovely lady who is married to a great man, Naaman, the Commander of the Army of the king of Aram no less. Unfortunately his skin is starting to go bad and there's no cure. However, I told my mistress about our prophet Elisha in Samaria, who would cure him because of his great faith in God. Well, she went and told Naaman who went to his king who gave him permission to go. He even gave him a letter to the king of Israel, plus silver, gold and clothing.

Well of course the king of Israel couldn't cure him and he got really mad but fortunately Elisha got to hear about it and sent for Naaman. When he got there though, Elisha only sent out a messenger telling him to go and wash 7 times in the River Jordan and he would be healed.

Naaman was angry, firstly because he thought Elisha should have come out and at least laid hands on him personally but also because the small and dirty Jordan was so beneath a man of his position, so he went off in a strop.

What a good job my friends, the other servants, put him wise. They tactfully suggested that he had too much pride! Naaman had calmed down and saw sense, went and dipped himself in the Jordan 7 times and he came back healed – his skin like that of a young boy!

He went back to thank Elisha and gave God the glory because he realised that it was the power of God that had healed him.

Well Mama, my master and mistress gave me some credit as well, as it was little old me that mentioned Elisha so I'm riding on a high at the moment.

I'm actually quite happy here Mama, so don't worry about me any more. Maybe they'll let me visit you one day.

God bless you and Daddy.

Love you lots.

Abi

2 Kings 5

Letter From a King's Cupbearer
(Joseph in Prison)

Greetings to my favourite Uncle,

You asked me recently to tell you about our latest big-shot here called Joseph, aka Zaphenath-Paneah – I'll call him Joseph, his Hebrew name, as his Egyptian name is a bit of a mouthful.

Well what you heard is all true but you may not have heard about his background which, as I know him well, is quite colourful. When we spent time in prison together he told me how he was a boastful teenager in the land of Canaan and how his brothers had sold him into slavery and he ended up in Egypt, sold to Potiphah, the Captain of the Guard. He was a very capable young man, learned our language and customs and was favoured by his God in everything he did so Potiphah put him in charge of his whole household for many years – trusted him with everything! Only fly in the ointment was Mrs Potiphah who really fancied him. Joe kept resisting her advances until one day her pride got the better of her and she accused him of 'messing with her'. Pot was blind with rage and threw Joe into prison without trial. However, even there his God blessed him and the warder put Joe in charge of everyone.

That was where I met him because Pharaoh had a hissy fit with me – his cupbearer – and his chief baker and put us in custody in Potiphah's prison. So, while there we both had peculiar dreams which Joe interpreted for us and which, within three days, came true. Fortunately for me I went back to work for Pharaoh but the baker was killed.

I also forgot all about Joe.

Anyway, two years later Pharaoh had a weird dream too but no-one could tell him what it meant. That rang a bell in my head so I told him about Joe's God giving him the interpretation of my dream so Joe was spruced up and brought before Pharaoh.

Well, Joe's God told him that the dream meant that there would be seven years of prosperity followed by seven years of famine – oh, and that someone wise and discerning should be in charge of the harvests, storage and distribution.

I had to laugh because I knew Joe was skilfully putting ideas into Pharaoh's head about who should be in charge and he succeeded! Joe's God had succeeded!

So this was how Joe, at 30 years old, became number one in the land after Pharaoh and has stored up so much grain in every city that we can sell it to all the starving nations that come here and beg for help. It's making Pharaoh very rich.

When you think about it Uncle, to bring Joseph from an arrogant young teenage slave to a wise and powerful governor of Egypt, his God must really be the number one God in heaven. I'm certainly thanking him for all He's done for me!

Come and visit soon and maybe I'll introduce you to my friend, if you're lucky.

Regards to Auntie and my Coz,

Hapsett

Genesis 37 - 41

Letter From an Egyptian Steward
(Joseph and His Brothers)

Dearest Sister Cleo,

Thought I'd give you all the gossip about my Master, Joseph – or strictly speaking – Zaphenath-Paneah.

Remember how I told you he'd come originally from Canaan, sold by his brothers into slavery and how he ended up as Governor of Egypt? Well, his family turned up recently!! Well, some of his brothers anyway, although I didn't know that at the time.

My Master kept accusing them – through a translator - of being spies but, every so often, I saw him turn away and have a sniffle into his hanky – I wondered what was up with him! He kept asking after their father and younger brother too. He put one brother in prison as a hostage and sent the others back to their old father with lots of provisions and Master told me to even put some silver in their sacks. They were to bring their younger brother back to Egypt.

So when they returned I was told to take them to our house and prepare a dinner for them. They seemed really worried about the silver I'd put in their bags so I told them it was their God who did it! When Master arrived he asked them lots more questions but when he saw the youngest brother he had to hurry out and find somewhere private to weep again.

Master again gave me instructions for when they left, some of which were pretty weird but I just got on with it – I guessed what he was doing by now. To cut a long story short, I had to accuse the younger brother of stealing in order to bring them all back, bowing down on their knees to him and begging for mercy which, apparently he had seen in a dream as a teenager and had upset his brothers so hugely.

Suddenly Master Joseph made all us servants leave the room but we could hear clearly through the door. Master had broken down completely and was sobbing his heart out. The brothers were terrified but he eventually told them he was the brother they had sold into slavery but that God had meant it to happen so that he could now save so many lives. Well, now they were all weeping and kissing and hugging and outside the door we were all doing the same!

Pharaoh was so pleased about all this that he told Master to send cartloads of food, clothes, money and loads of donkeys to bring back the father and all his family and servants to come and live nearby in a fertile piece of land called Goshen.

Gosh Sis, it's been a real emotional roller-coaster and I'm sure someone will write a tome about it one day and I think this God of his will have his hand upon our future here.

Give my love to the family,

Abdul

Genesis 42 - 47

Letter from a Leper
(The Ten Lepers)

Greetings to my old friend Ezra.

You may be surprised to hear from me and when I tell you what's happened to me, you'll be even more amazed that I am writing this with my own hand.

Since we last met, I developed the ghastly skin disease, leprosy, and have had to live in a colony with other lepers, separate from everyone I know and love. The nerves in my fingers and toes were affected so badly I couldn't walk or even feed myself properly, so have been living off the charity of others.

Well, when we heard that the man, Jesus, was coming through town on his way to Jerusalem, ten of us, who had heard about his healing powers, went out and stood near the road hoping to catch a glimpse of him. We all called out to him saying, "Jesus, Master, have pity on us".

To our astonishment and delight he said, "Go, show yourselves to the priests!"

Well, normally we wouldn't do that until after our leprosy went into remission – if it ever did – so that we had permission to go home, but this Jesus was telling us to go now!

Well Ezra, I only had a tiny bit of faith and I didn't know if this would be OK with the priests, but we all went and, guess what, we were healed on our way! My fingers and toes grew back and my skin looked like a baby's. The priests said we were clean again.

I was so grateful that I hurried back to find Jesus to thank him, and I threw myself at his feet praising God, but Jesus asked,

"Were not all ten cleansed? Where are the other nine? Was no-one found to return to give praise to God except this foreigner?"

I realised then that, somehow, he knew I was a Samaritan, a race despised by Jews, but I guess God's grace is for everyone. Jesus then said,

"Rise and go, your faith has made you well."

I'm so glad I was obedient and acted on the little faith I had, and I'm glad I came back to thank him too 'cause I could see this pleased Jesus.

So, Ezra, now you know how I came to be writing this, and I recommend that when Jesus visits your town, you get out to hear what he says 'cause he truly has God's power in him.

Your pal, Micah

Luke 17: 11-19

Letter From a Little Boy
(Loaves and Fishes)

Dear Uncle Felix,

Thought I'd write and tell you what happened to me yesterday – it was so amazing!

I'd gone with a huge crowd to hear the man Jesus speak and Mum had packed me a lunch box 'cause she knew it could be ages before I got home.

Well, we were all flagging a bit in the heat but I'd managed to get near the front so I heard Jesus tell his friends to feed us. We all looked at one another in bewilderment 'cause here we were on a mountain, a long way from any bakeries and his friends were questioning Jesus as to just how were they to feed such a humongous crowd - think of the expense anyway!

Well, Uncle, I can't remember exactly whether I got my lunch out to eat MY snack or whether, without thinking, I offered to share it with someone but suddenly one of Jesus' friends grabbed it and showed it to Jesus saying "Here's a lad with 5 little barley loaves and 2 little fishes" then Jesus took it – took MY food!

He lifted it up and I think he praised God and blessed it then said something which I thought was a bit daft – he told his friends to share it around – my little lunch to more than 5000 people!

But, Uncle Felix, somehow, miraculously, unbelievably, we all had enough to eat!

I couldn't wait to get home and tell Mum what her little packed lunch had been able to do – (she didn't believe me until our neighbours said I wasn't fibbing.)

But, d'you know, there was lots left over – how did Jesus do that? If people hadn't believed before that he had God's power in him, they certainly did now!

I might not remember all that he spoke about but I know for sure that, even if we only have a little of anything, it can be used for great things if we offer it up to God and share it.

Come and have dinner with us one day Uncle Felix, I'm quite sure we'll have enough to go around.

Love

Solomon

John 6

Letter From a Lost Son
(The Prodigal Son)

Dear Dad,

I don't suppose you ever thought you'd hear from me again and, after what I've done you may not want to. I wouldn't blame you if you even throw this letter away without reading it.

I've been a really stupid, arrogant wastrel of a son and I've got no excuse. I suppose I was plain greedy, thinking of my inheritance and all the things I could get with it.

When you gave me my share I didn't give my older brother a thought – I just assumed he would stay and work for you and look after you. I only thought of the moment and selfishly left you both to go and enjoy myself. What you don't know, Dad, is that I blew the whole lot in wild living – everyone wanted to be my friend and share my wealth. I got taken for a ride but I also did a lot of things that I was not brought up to do. It all went to my head very quickly.

Unfortunately, Dad, at the same time that I spent it all there was a famine and I couldn't find work and had no money to buy food even if I lived rough.

Oh Dad, I was starting to regret my actions but then I got a job, only to be sent to his fields to feed his pigs! You know, Dad, what us Jews think about pigs, and here was I amongst them!

But worse still I was so hungry that I started looking amongst the pig-swill to find something to fill my empty belly.

Oh the shame of it, Dad. I had got to rock-bottom and even thought of suicide.

Then I came to my senses and thought that even your hired hands probably have something to eat and are not starving to death like me.

But it wasn't just my empty belly that was in need – I just felt so ashamed of what I must've put you through, Dad. I realised what a horrible person I had become, sinning against you and God. I suddenly realised that I needed your forgiveness but I had to go back home to ask for it.

I know I am no longer worthy to be called your son but if you could find it in your heart to forgive me I would also beg you to let me work for you as a hired hand.

Of course, Dad, you may have disowned me long ago and consider me lost and dead to you, and want nothing more to do with me, and I don't blame you, but at the end of the day I am hoping God will enable you to forgive me and be compassionate to me.

Whatever you decide, Dad, I love you and I'm coming home to you.

Yours, unworthily,

Your dear son

Luke 15: 11

Letter from a Man with Good Friends
(Paralytic on the Roof)

To my dear brother Moshe,

Thought I'd let you know what extra special friends I've got and how their faith, love and concern for me has helped to change my life.

When we all heard that Jesus of Nazareth was coming to town my friends decided to take me to him and ask him to heal me. They knew, like you, brother, that I've been paralysed for ever, and so with no muscles to walk at all, they had to carry me to the house where he was speaking to hundreds of people including the teachers of the law. However, when we arrived, we couldn't get in but my friends didn't give up – they carried me up the outside stairs to the roof and proceeded to dig a hole above the room where Jesus was! I was shaking with a mixture of excitement and fear – would someone stop them? Would they get through? Would they get me through?

Suddenly I could see Jesus looking up at me as my friends lowered me down through the hole right in front of him. From a stunned silence, the crowd erupted! Then Jesus bent over me with such compassion in his eyes that I thought he was looking right into my soul.

"Friend, your sins are forgiven," he said. Woah! That upset the religious ones, as we all knew that only God has power to forgive our sins. Jesus saw their reaction and asked whether it was easier to say "Your sins are forgiven" or "Get up and walk" Of course, the teachers were purple with fury and screaming "Blasphemy!" Jesus was claiming something outrageous! So, to prove to them that he had God's authority to do both he told me to get up, pick up my mat and go home! Everyone held their breath. The silence was deafening.

Well Moshe, if I'd had any muscles they'd have turned to jelly then, but, somehow, I knew that I had been healed. My whole body felt different – strong even, so I slowly straightened my legs and pushed myself up until

I was standing before Jesus. My friends, who had jumped down the hole above, threw their arms around me and everyone cheered and whooped and, as they recognised that Jesus was the Messiah – able to heal the body and save the soul – they praised God like I've never heard before.

I picked up my mat, mouthed a "Thank you" to a smiling Jesus and eventually we went home.

So, Moshe, I'll walk round to see you soon and show you what God has done.

From your very happy and healthy brother,

Amos

Matthew 9 and Luke 5

Letter from Martha's Neighbour
(Raising of Lazarus)

To My Dear Friend Joanna,

Gosh I don't know where to start!

OK, you've met my neighbours, Mary, Martha and Lazarus haven't you? Well, the other week Lazarus became ill and they sent a message to their friend, Jesus, the man who claims to be from God. They probably thought that he would come straightaway and heal him but he didn't! He wasn't many miles away and could've come apparently but chose not to, but then, when he decided the time was right, he did. Unfortunately he was too late and Lazarus had popped his clogs. He was wrapped in burial cloths and put in a tomb in a nearby cave and they put a stone slab across the entrance.

Martha told me later that when she and Mary went out to meet Jesus he cried with them, which was lovely that he showed his grief, as not many men do in public. However, when they all reached the tomb he told them to take away the stone! Martha pointed out that, as Lazarus had been there four days, there would be a nasty pong but she obeyed anyway.

Then Jesus looked up and thanked God for hearing him, then called out very loudly,

"Lazarus, come out!"

There was a deafening silence from the crowd. I was as shocked as anyone – could he? Would he?

Then – oh my goodness, this white apparition came stumbling out of the cave, still wrapped up like a mummy. Jesus told them to take off the graveclothes and there stood Lazarus – alive and well – and he didn't pong!

You should've heard the cheering and clapping, Jo. We all wanted to go and touch Lazarus to make sure he was real and not a ghost.

Martha explained to me later that Jesus knew he could come and heal the sickness but wanted to demonstrate God's power and love through him by raising him from the dead.

I now believe that if my prayers aren't answered straightaway there's a bloomin' good reason and I just need to thank God for hearing me and trust him for the right time.

Hope to see you soon, Jo.

Love Sarah

John 11

Letter From a "Once-Blind" Man
(Healing of a Blind Man)

Greetings Brother,

As you know I was born blind and so I've never learned to write so our local scribe is writing this for me.

I don't know if you've heard from Mother and Father lately so I'm telling you my version of what's happened to me recently. It's so amazing you'd better sit down.

One Sabbath as I was sitting by the side of the road, hoping for a few coins from the caring, I heard men discussing my blindness and whether I or Mum and Dad were sinners that I was born blind. The man they called Jesus denied it and put them right.

Suddenly I heard him spit – yes spit! I heard someone say he was using the mud to make clay – which is forbidden on the Sabbath but I certainly wasn't expecting him to splodge it on my eyes – whoa! However, I've had worse on me and this Jesus seemed so gentle and compassionate that I didn't struggle. Then he said,

"Go, wash in the Pool of Siloam", so some people showed me the way there and I washed the mud off my eyes. As I did so everything became light and I remembered Jesus saying that he was the light of the world. Then I could see things moving and I knew that Jesus had healed my blindness. It was so overwhelming as I didn't know what things were – only what they felt and sounded like. My neighbours couldn't believe it was me but I said it was me and told them what happened but I couldn't take them to Jesus because I didn't know what he looked like.

Well, what a commotion! They took me to the Pharisees but instead of them being pleased they were fuming because healing wasn't allowed on the Sabbath either.

They even sent for our parents to prove that I had been born blind but they were so fearful of excommunication they said I could speak for myself.

The Pharisees wanted me to deny Jesus but I wasn't interested in their games – I stuck to the facts – once I was blind, now I see! Because they couldn't argue with the facts they were furious. I got a bit cheeky at that point and asked if they wanted to become Jesus' disciples! I felt bold enough to challenge their arguments – me! A beggar! You would have been proud of me Brother.

But then I was cursed and evicted from the synagogue but I didn't care – I was healed and I knew the truth of it. Well Jesus heard about my eviction and came and found me, but, of course, as I hadn't seen him I had no idea who he was. But he told me he was the Son of Man and I told him I believed him.

To cap it all Jesus told the Pharisees that they were blind and guilty if they weren't open to see the truth of who he is.

If you come and visit I'll be able to see you, Brother, for the first time in my life – won't that be something!

Regards,

Solomon

John 9

Letter From a Pilgrim
(The Coming of the Holy Spirit)

Greetings Cousin,

As you know I came to Jerusalem to celebrate Passover and stayed for (Pentecost) the Feast of Weeks, to thank God for our wonderful harvest, but something has happened here so I decided to stay longer. Let me explain:

First thing in the morning of the Feast day I was walking, along with crowds of other Jewish foreigners, past a house where there was such a commotion I stopped to listen. There I heard someone praising and declaring the wonders of God in my own language! Mesopotamian! Others around me seemed to be hearing their own tongue as well, how amazing was that? What an attention-getter! However some seemed to be saying that they were drunk but a man called Peter stood up and explained that it was only 9 in the morning and they were fasting anyway at their early prayer meeting – No, it was the promised Holy Spirit, he said, that had been foretold by the prophet Joel. He then went on about Jesus the Nazarene who claimed to be the Son of God and did lots of miraculous things and who had been crucified 50 days earlier at Passover.

Well, cousin, I had been there at that time but I hadn't realised the significance of it or even believed the rumours that the man had come back to life and had appeared before his followers and lots of others, teaching them and even eating with them!

So this Peter was saying that Jesus had now gone back to heaven but promised to send the Holy Spirit to everyone who believed in him and were truly sorry for their wicked ways. I was a God-fearing Jew but it was as if my eyes were suddenly opened to the truth of what I was really like and I felt as if I was seeing myself as God saw me – and I didn't like it so I found myself weeping and saying sorry – I even fell on my knees in the dust and didn't care what anyone else thought, although I think others were doing the same. After a while I found myself laughing, uncontrollably and as I stood up I hugged the man next to me and we jumped around together like a couple of mad men, as if we were now drunk! One of the disciples came over and explained that we also had received the gift of God's Holy Spirit and I realised there were hundreds, no, thousands of us all in the same boat. Wow! Since that day we've all been meeting and eating together and hearing all the things that Jesus told his friends while he was with them – it's mind blowing – I shall never be the same you know! Everywhere the disciples go people are being healed but the priests, religious leaders and temple guards are now getting a tad unhappy because they are scared of losing control of the masses and, despite the awesome atmosphere and so much praising God, there is this undercurrent that not everyone is happy with the situation.

So I think it's time I made my way home soon but I am a different person now which is why I'm sending you this message so you can be prepared for anything I might do or say when I get back. God be with you,

Haran

Acts 2-3

Letter from a Refugee
(Mary and Joseph's Flight to Egypt)

Greetings Dear Cousin Elizabeth,

I hope you get this message OK as it has a long way to travel and it cost me a fortune to find the right man to take it.

I'm writing to tell you that Joseph and I have brought our little son out of harms way to Egypt but, first things first. After he was born, when the census crowds had gone home, we managed to find a little place to rent so that we could go through all the rituals like circumcision, (we named him Jesus like the angel said) and presenting him to God at the Temple. (Remind me later to tell you the amazing words from a lovely old man called Simeon. God had revealed to him who our baby boy really is and what he would become – they were almost the same things that you said to me when I came to visit you in your pregnancy!) Then I had to be ceremonially cleansed by offering sacrifices of doves to the priests, as is our custom. Then we planned to return home.

Well, as you probably know, dearest Lizzy, King Herod had heard from the wise men, who eventually found us in Bethlehem, that a new king had been born and Herod was so scared that he would lose his throne that he ordered the killing of all the little Jewish boys under two years of age. I'm glad the wise men had the gumption to go straight back home and not tell him where we were.

Anyway, that was when Joseph had an amazing dream, when an angel of the Lord appeared to him and told him to take me and Jesus to Egypt as King Herod was searching for him. Now Joe is a good and righteous man and knew God was guiding him so when he woke me and told me to get up, we scrambled around to collect a few things in bags, including the beautiful gifts the wise men had given us and just upped and went – on our one and only donkey! We had no time to go shopping so it was an awful journey with just the basics for surviving. Poor Joe had so many blisters and our tummies rumbled most of the time. Strange isn't it that centuries earlier our ancestors went to Egypt because of a famine and remained there for ages? God saved them and I know he'll save us too but I hope we come home a bit sooner than them!

Well, Lizzy, we've found a colony of Jews in this city so we'll wait here until God moves us onwards or back to our homeland. I wonder how we'll hear – it may be an angel again. I'll try and get a message to you when we do.

Give my love to Zechariah and your little boy, John. I long to see you all again.

Mary

Matthew 2

Letter from a Rich Ruler
(The Rich Young Ruler)

Greetings My Dear Friend Matthew,

As we've been friends a long time I'll get straight to the point. I'm so shocked and saddened at something that the Rabbi Jesus said to me I need a second opinion.

When I met him recently, he was talking about eternal life so I came right out and asked him what I had to do to inherit eternal life. As I expected he said to obey the 10 Commandments so I told him I had kept them since I was a boy so I was expecting him to say that I was all right then.

However, he then said something so unexpected it really wiped the smug smile off my face – he told me to sell everything and give it to the poor and I would have treasure in heaven! Then I should follow him! Sell everything Matt! Well you know how much money, property and possessions I have and how much power and prestige I enjoy. I was so dumbfounded I couldn't speak.

Other people who were listening saw my dilemma and even though he hadn't told them to sell everything, they asked if, because they'd done their best, who on earth could be saved?

Then Jesus said how hard it is for the rich to enter the kingdom of God – impossible for people like me who are so secure in our wealth but possible if we trust our lives and future with God.

One of his followers, Simon Peter, said that he'd left everything – his home, family and job – to follow him so Jesus reminded him that he would receive many times as much in this age and in the age to come – eternal life.

So Jesus left – and I didn't follow him.

My heart was telling me that I was not satisfied with all my riches – my life wasn't empty but something was missing. However, my head just couldn't balance the sacrifice and the benefit. There's just too much to give up – working all my life to get where I am. Anyway, why didn't he tell everyone else to do the same?

Matt, you know me, do you think I put my wealth, status and reputation before God? No, don't answer that – just tell me what you would have done. Perhaps we could discuss this when you come round to my banquet next week – I'll have a nice roast ready for us and I've got a new batch of wine in too.

Your dear friend

Thomas

Luke 18: 18

Letter from a Roman Soldier
(The Crucifixion)

Greetings Brother,

You may be wondering what all the fuss is about in Jerusalem where I work for the Roman Governor, Pontius Pilate, so I'm letting you know of a big miscarriage of justice that I was part of.

We had two men in custody, one was Yeshua Bar-Abbas (Jesus Barabbas) and the other was Yeshua ha-Notzri (Jesus of Nazareth). In fact both were called Son of the Father but the difference was that Barabbas wanted to free Israel from us Romans by force and the other wanted to free Israel using non-violence.

Poor old Pilate couldn't find any legal crime that warranted Jesus of Nazareth's execution so just had him flogged and was then going to release him but unfortunately it was our custom to release a prisoner during the Jewish holidays and as it was Passover, he asked the crowd outside who he should set free. The crowd kept shouting for Barabbas – the one who was really guilty of murder and rebellion – and they got louder and louder, even I was a bit scared!

They wanted Jesus of Nazareth to die - "Crucify him, crucify him!" they kept screaming – my word, what an angry mob. The suspense was awful but eventually Pilate gave in – I think he was scared of losing his job at that point.

And so, the innocent Jesus of Nazareth was taken by me and my fellow soldiers and crucified brutally and painfully on a cross. He died in the place of Barabbas, who was set free.

Some of my mates were mocking Jesus but in my heart I just knew there was so much more to this man's death. He had claimed to be the Jewish Messiah, the Son of God no less and when he was dying up there on the cross, the ground shook and it all went dark for three hours – it was really spooky! I wondered if his God was so angry he would wipe us all out, even my boss remarked that Jesus was indeed the Son of God.

Normally we have to go and break the bones of the criminals, just to make sure they were dead but we could see that Jesus was already dead. However, I was ordered to pierce his side with my spear. I was shaking like crazy but I had to obey my superior officer and the spear brought a flow of blood and water so I knew he was definitely dead now.

Well, Bruv, I've heard his body had been put securely in a tomb but I've also heard that it's not there anymore, and that people have seen him alive again but I can assure you my spear proved he was dead. However, it's making me wonder…

I'm sure I'll have more to tell you next time I write.

Regards to your dear wife and kiddies,

Your brother Andreas

Matt 27, Luke 23, John 19

Letter From a Sea Captain
(Jonah and the Whale)

Greetings Cousin Laban,

It is a long time since you've heard from me as I am away at sea such a lot but I just had to tell you about one of my passengers.

The man, Jonah, came aboard at Joppa and it wasn't long before a gale sprang up. I say 'gale' but it turned into a really scary violent storm, the likes of which I'd not encountered before.

Every man was calling out to his god and we'd chucked a lot of heavy stuff overboard, neither of which made any difference.

The passenger, Jonah, had managed to go to sleep below deck so I woke him up and told him to call on his god too. Then the crew cast lots to find out who was responsible for the storm and it seemed to be Jonah who was the cause of all the trouble.

We asked him what he had done and he said he was a Hebrew and he was running away from his God, the Creator of all. He said he was to blame and we should throw him overboard!

Well we didn't really want to but, crying out to Jonah's God, we tossed him over and the wind died down! Wow! Well we really believed in his God then but that's not the end of the story, Laban, because I heard later that he was alive! Not only that but he had been swallowed up by a big fish and three days later had been spat out alive on to the beach! Coo I bet he ponged.

Apparently, his God could hear his prayers from inside the fish! None of our gods would hear us, be merciful and deliver us like that.

Also, I heard that Jonah had eventually obeyed his God by going back to Ninevah and all the people there believed in him too.

I like the sound of a God who is interested in us and cares about our every move, don't you?

Will try and get to visit you when I'm next ashore,

Best wishes,

Silas

Jonah 1

Letter from a Secret Believer
(Being Born Again)

Greetings to my old friend Reuel,

In reply to your letter about the man, Jesus of Nazareth, I will tell you something I haven't told anyone else – yet.

As you know I am a Pharisee and a member of the ruling council so I consider myself pretty religious and well educated as we debate and discuss all sorts of stuff and uphold laws but Jesus often criticised us for being hypocrites and challenged our views – no-one had ever done that so openly before and his boldness and authority really made me question our laws and motives.

One evening I had such an urge inside me to find out more about Jesus – I wanted, no, needed answers so I put my fear (of my peers) and my pride aside and, once it was dark I went to see him with an open mind to separate fact from fiction.

First thing he said was really odd – I couldn't enter the kingdom of heaven unless I was born again! How ridiculous did that sound?

Well, my knowledge was that the kingdom would be ruled by God, restored on earth and us religious ones would be a part of it but Jesus went on to explain that it was a personal thing and the entrance requirements are repentance and spiritual rebirth and that it had already begun in the hearts of true believers. He said he hadn't come to condemn the world but to save it if only we believed in him.

I knew the Scriptures but I didn't know God personally or his gift of salvation.

Well, Reuel, I went home almost singing, I felt excited by this new understanding and a feeling that I could be liberated from man's suffocating religious laws.

However, I kept quiet about it at the Council meetings until one day they wanted to arrest Jesus but the temple guards couldn't find any reason to and reported back that he was speaking with authority and doing good things like miracles. My mates were getting really hot under the collar but I suddenly spoke out! I knew I was risking my reputation and high position but I knew we needed to hear what he said before we condemned him. First they looked shocked then they scowled but I didn't actually say I was a believer.

Well, to cut a long story short, Jesus was finally arrested then tried before Pontius Pilate and finally crucified, all within such a short space of time. I couldn't believe it – it didn't seem right – or real.

My mate on the Council, Joseph of Aramathea, who also secretly believed, asked Pilate for Jesus' body and, with me, quietly carried him away. I had brought along a mixture of myrrh and aloes and we wrapped Jesus, with the spices, in strips of linen and carried him into a cave cut in the hillside (I think it may have been ready for Joseph's burial) and rolled a huge stone in front of the entrance, then we scarpered as it was getting dark and the Sabbath Day was approaching.

Now Reuel, you may not believe this, but his disciples are saying that his body disappeared and, not only that, they say they've seen him and he's talked to them!

Now I know what I know – that man was dead! I would have known if he'd just been unconscious – he was dead!

Anyway Joseph and I are going to meet up with his disciples soon and I am so excited I can't tell you!

Why don't you come and visit and catch my excitement?

And bring the family!

Your friend, Nicodemus

John 3: 1-21; 7: 50-52; 19: 39-40

Letter from a Shield-Bearer
(David and Goliath)

Greetings Cousin Hezrob,

I thought I'd let you know that I am home safe from the awful battle we Philistines had with the Israelites and, goodness, Hez, I only just escaped with my life.

I call it a battle but it really was a strange and awesome show-down. As you know we are a very tall and hefty people and we were facing their King Saul's puny army across the valley. I have been Goliath's shield-bearer for some time now but not only is his shield heavy, I have to go ahead of him – very privileged but also very risky.

Well, for forty days Goliath and I went forward, down our hill, every morning and evening, taunting the Israelites, calling for their best soldier to fight him so that whoever survived could win the battle. It was funny to watch those poor little terrified Israelites run back up their hill.

Eventually we saw a young lad coming towards us but he wasn't wearing any armour or carrying any weapons, just a staff in his hands! When he neared the stream in front of us, he bent down, picked up some stones and we all moved closer and closer. Well, I was chuckling as I handed Goliath his shield but he seemed to be angry and started cursing this young lad who didn't seem scared or intimidated at all.

In fact, the boy said he was coming against Goliath in the name of the Lord Almighty, the God of the armies of Israel and that he would strike him down and cut off his head and feed all us Philistines to the birds and the beasts so that the whole world would know that there is a God in Israel. He said that everyone would know that it's not by sword or spear that the Lord saves, for the battle is the Lord's and he would give us all into their hands! We were all laughing at his audacity as we moved closer but then this lad reached into his bag, took out a stone, put it into a sling, quickly slung it and struck Goliath on his forehead, killing him instantly!

I was in shock but the boy ran over, stood over the body, took hold of Goliath's sword and cut his head off! Boy, did I run at that point as the Israelites charged forward and chased us all the way back to Gath and Ekron. I don't quite know how I escaped, I guess I can run quickly if I have to.

Well, I heard later that the young lad, who was called David, was given King Saul's daughter in marriage as a reward so I reckon we'll hear more of him and his God one day.

It just goes to show he was right – that with his God on his side it didn't matter how big his enemy was. Maybe we need to think about that, Hez, and quietly find out more about David's God.

Best wishes to your family,

Zog

1 Samuel 17

Letter from a Tax Collector
(Zacchaeus)

My Dear Friend Malachi,

You'll never guess what happened to me recently! - I met the celebrated prophet Jesus! And not only that, he asked if he could come to tea – actually he didn't ask, he just told me he was coming to stay at my house! Well, I nearly fell off my perch! Why perch? You may well ask. Well, I suppose I'd better start at the beginning 'cos you're sure not gonna believe the ending!

Like I said, I was in Jericho, minding my own business and collecting everybody else's taxes when I heard that the man Jesus was gonna pass through town on his way to Jerusalem, I think.

Well, like everyone else, I wanted to see this celeb – I wondered what made him different, what had given him a reputation as a healer and rebel. So I joined the crowd but, as you know Mal, I'm on the short side so I couldn't see a thing. People don't like me Mal, 'cos, like you, I'm a tax collector par excellence, so I couldn't ask to look out of their high window or balcony. But there was a tree which looked sturdy enough to bear my weight so up I shinned. No sooner than I peered out from the leaves than Jesus came along.

Well, Mal, you just wouldn't believe what happened next. Just as Jesus got to the tree he looked up at me with his piercingly beautiful eyes – yes I know Mal, men aren't supposed to say things like that but you should've seen them! Anyway, he said "Zacchaeus" – yes, he knew my name! He called to me by my name! How did he know that? Anyway, he said "Zacchaeus, come down immediately, I must stay at your house today!"

Well, Mal, like I said, I nearly fell off my perch! Although I was shocked that he knew me I was even more shocked that he wanted to stay at my house! Me – a tax collector, despised and hated by everyone just for doing my job. But Jesus didn't seem to despise me – in fact what happened next will blow your mind Mal. As I climbed down, all the people were muttering and berating Jesus for being the guest of a sinner but this Jesus didn't bat an eyelid. He didn't care for convention, he was a compassionate radical with a mind of his own.

Well, Mal, I'm not sure what happened next but I think I suddenly saw myself as Jesus saw me – and I just knew I was a sinner – I often took more taxes than was necessary and cheated people – well we all had perks didn't we? And suddenly I was blurting out that there and then I was going to give half my possessions to the poor and that if I had cheated anyone (which of course I knew I had) then I would pay back four times the amount!

Are you still reading this Mal? Yes, this was me, your friend and fellow tax collector Zacchaeus, saying all this and the people around me were either gobsmacked and frowning or cheering for me.

Anyway, I must've said something right 'cos next thing, Jesus said, "Today, salvation has come to this house, because this man, too, is a son of Abraham." Then he said that the Son of Man came to seek and save the lost. Well, he did come to stay and my servants dished up dinner and I let them stay and listen to all that Jesus said. He convinced us all, Mal, that Yahweh has sent him to save the world although I didn't understand that fully. But he said me and my household were saved.

Have I freaked you out, Mal? If you haven't fallen off your chair, would you like to come and stay at my house too so I can tell you all the rest that Jesus said – it's life-changing, as you can tell!

Regards to your dear wife Anna,

Your friend Zac

Luke 19: 1-10

Letter from a Taxi Driver
(Philip and the Eunuch)

To my dear sister Chloe,

When I last saw you I was about to take a very important man in my chariot from our home in Ethiopia to the big city of the Jews, Jerusalem, in Judea.

Well I can tell you now, it was none other than the Treasurer of our Queen, Candace! He wanted to worship the Jewish God in Jerusalem and as I am known for my wonderful driving skills I was chosen to take Euny (I call him that but not to his face of course - heaven forbid!)

We got to know each other quite well on our long journey even though he is so important and I am a nobody who will never be remembered. On the way to the city he had been reading from the Jewish Scriptures, from the book of the prophet Isaiah and he told me that the prophet says encouraging words to foreigners and eunuchs. However, on the way back he was reading from another chapter, out loud because he says he can concentrate better - although I think it's because he wants me to hear and convert to his faith.

Anyway, this man suddenly appeared, jogging beside us and asked Euny if he understood what he was reading. What a nerve! But Euny admitted that nobody had ever explained it to him and invited the man, who introduced himself as Philip, to jump up and join him. He'd been reading about a sheep going to the slaughter and a lamb being silent and Philip explained it was a prophetic reference to the man Jesus of Nazareth, the Lamb of God, who'd been sacrificed and crucified for claiming to be the Son of God. Philip said those who believed this Jesus and were baptised as an outward sign, would have their sins forgiven and look forward to everlasting life!

Obviously I couldn't help earwigging and it was fascinating stuff but I was stunned when Euny told me to stop as he wanted to be baptised in the little stream we were passing. Out they jumped and I was the only witness to Philip dunking Euny under the water in his underwear! When I next looked round Philip had disappeared and Euny got back in the chariot - wet but ecstatically happy and we both sang out hearts out all the way home.

Since we got back I've heard that Euny's been telling everyone about Jesus the Messiah and loads of people have believed and been baptised.

Who knows, Chloe, I might be next. Come and visit as soon as possible so I can tell you all about Jesus too.

Fondest love from

Your Brother Sam.

Acts 9 : 6-39 and Isaiah 56 and 53.

Letter from a Temple Teacher
(Jesus aged 12)

Greetings Mother,

I'm sorry you couldn't get to the Passover Feast this week but as something unusual happened in the temple the other day, I thought you might be interested, especially as you're a parent and all that.

Many people had left, as they had travelled a long way but we rabbis and teachers were still in the temple courts discussing, sometimes quite heatedly, our Scriptures and laws, as we often do.

There was a lad there, about twelve years old, who was extremely knowledgeable about spiritual matters – and it wasn't all head knowledge, his heart was really in it as he debated like an adult. In fact, we were sometimes stunned by his wisdom and understanding.

Anyway, at some point his parents showed up and, in front of us all, they gave him a right ear bashing about how they had been searching for him for three days. Apparently, they had headed home to Nazareth with all their relatives and Mum thought the lad was with Dad and visa versa and when they realised he was missing they had to come back to Jerusalem and search among the crowds for him.

This lad, who they called Jesus, gave such an odd reply, a question and an answer together that none of us understood.

"Why were you searching for me? Didn't you know I had to be in my Father's house?"

Our jaws all dropped at this young whipper-snapper's words to his parents. I thought of you, Mother, and how you would have boxed my ears if I had spoken to you like that but they just looked at each other as if they knew something we didn't. Then Jesus got up, said thank you and goodbye to us and went off with his parents.

I've thought a lot about this lad since then, the way he was so at ease in God's temple and as if there was something special about him. I wonder if he will turn up one day as a chief rabbi – I must keep my eye open for him.

I trust you will be well enough to get to the next Feast, Mother.

From your loving son,

Joel

Luke 2: 41-52

Letter from a Wedding Guest
(Water into Wine)

Greetings Nephew,

It was good to see you the other week but what a pity you couldn't stay for the wedding. However, a week-long festival wouldn't help your business. I must tell you though of something amazing that happened while I was there.

Do you remember that Mary, her son Jesus and his friends had been invited (along with half the town of course) well, at some point I overheard Mary tell Jesus that we'd drunk all the wine and I was curious as to what Jesus would reply, after all, our unwritten laws of hospitality are pretty well known.

As I thought, it was a negative reply which I didn't really understand (something about it not being his time) but then Mary, without batting an eyelid, told the servants to do whatever Jesus told them. (Did she know something that I didn't?) I thought maybe they would have a whip-round and go and buy more from the next village or something but Jesus told his servants to go and fill up the six nearby stone water jars. They looked at each other uncertainly, after all, the jars were huge, but then they obeyed him. Then he told them to fill up the wine jugs with the water and take them to the host.

I followed them because I wanted to see if he would spit the water out and become angry.

"What's this" he said to the servants who were quaking in their sandals. But before they could think of any reply the host called out to the bridegroom, "Normally we have the fine wines first" (after which we're too sozzled to notice) "But you've saved the best until now!" and we all gave a cheer and filled up our goblets! It was tasty too and so smooth. Jesus had saved the day and no-one would be embarrassed now.

I heard talk afterwards that Jesus was gathering a group of people who believed that he was the Son of God, the Messiah, the Chosen One, and, after seeing what happened to the water and wine, I'm starting to believe in him myself. Surely only God's power could do that?

Pity you missed it but I've got a feeling we'll see more things like that from Jesus.

Regards to your family,

Silas

John 2: 1-11

Letter from a Witness
(The Stoning of Stephen)

A message to my fellow disciple Nicholas,

As you have had to go home to your ailing parents in Antioch I thought I'd better put you in the picture regarding our dear brother in Christ, Stephen.

When you left you were aware of how close he was to God and how hard working he was for our Lord Jesus. You are now aware that I am using the past tense to tell you about what has happened to him.

Shortly after you went, some jealous opponents told lies about him, accusing him of blasphemy and it resulted in him being dragged before the religious leaders of the Sanhedrin to explain. I managed to stand at the back of the crowd and witnessed everything. You should have seen him, Nick, his face shone as the Holy Spirit filled him with peace and gave him shedloads of words to say.

He started with Abraham and told of the relationship and covenant that God has with his people and how we, as a nation, have disobeyed him so many times and rejected his prophets of old and now they had killed Jesus, the Messiah. Stephen used such strong language to them, no wonder they were going purple in the face and trying to cover their ears! Oh my goodness he really laid into them and yet he did it in a way that would have made Jesus proud.

Then he went a step too far for them – he looked up to heaven with a rapturous look on his face and said he could see heaven open and Jesus standing at the right hand of God! Oh what a privilege for him.

Well, it was obvious they weren't going to stand for that, and in their fury, they dragged him out of the city without even a trial and began to stone him! All our brothers were trying to stop them but there were too many of them and they were just like a pack of wolves tearing into their prey.

At one point I managed to get close enough to Stephen to hear him pray, "Lord Jesus, receive my spirit", then, under the onslaught of stones, he fell on his knees and cried out "Lord, do not hold this sin against them." It was just as if he was remembering the words that Jesus said when he was dying. He just lay there, covered in blood, until they realised that he was dead and then they slunk off silently. I was expecting a bolt of lightning or something but heaven was quiet, although I suspect that, as we were weeping for Stephen, Jesus and his angels were lifting him up into their arms.

I don't know what will happen now Nick so will write again soon.

Your dear friend, Parmenas

Acts 6 and 7

Letter From a Wounded Man
(Arrest of Jesus)

My Dear Brother Nathan,

I'm writing this in case you had heard rumours about me and I thought I'd tell you first-hand that I am totally OK.

What happened was because, as you know, I am Malchus, bond-servant of the High Priest Caiaphas, and I had been sent to arrest the rabbi Jesus who, Caiaphas said, was a dangerous rebel, leading the people astray. He was afraid to arrest him during the daytime because he thought it would cause a riot so I was sent under the cover of darkness although, with the temple guards and a cohort of Roman soldiers, all with torches, lanterns and weapons, it was quite a bright procession over the Kidron valley and into the olive grove where we suspected Jesus would be in hiding.

However, Jesus made it easy for us, stepping forwards and asking who we were looking for. When I said "Jesus of Nazareth" he answered "I AM". As he spoke, we all fell backwards on to the ground! I knew that was the name of Jehovah but the power as Jesus said it was something else!

Well, although we had only come for Jesus and not his disciples, one of them named Simon Peter drew his sword and tried to kill me but because he's a fisherman and not a swordsman, he missed my head but chopped my ear off!

So, I was in shock, pain, bleeding and wondering if I was going to die when Jesus reached forward, touched my ear and healed it completely. Me, who had gone there to arrest this dangerous man, gets his ear put back on. Well, I had heard about his miracles but I didn't believe them until it was me he healed.

Then, with authority, he told Simon Peter to put his sword away saying didn't he think he could call upon 12 legions of angels to save him and that the Scriptures say it has to be this way? It seemed like this arrested man was now in charge of his own destiny and I was just a pawn in some awful dark game. Me, the Chief Priest's ambassador had been used by the powers of darkness.

As I led him back into the city he caused me no problems – it was as if he knew what was coming next, whatever that might be. I felt dreadful because I could see this Jesus was such a kingly man yet so humble and full of grace and mercy that his followers were willing to die for him.

I think I'll be writing to you again soon Nathan, to tell you more about this amazing rabbi. Maybe I'll find out what else the Scriptures say.

Your loving brother,

Malchus

John 18

Letter from the Queen of Sheba
(Solomon and Sheba)

To my Dear Cousin Hannah,

I'm back now from my visit to the famous King Solomon, son of the equally famous King David of Israel and I have to tell you that everything we had heard about him is true – times 10!

It was a long and tiring journey to Jerusalem but we were all made very welcome – and comfortable, in his magnificent and extravagant palace – and you should have seen his new temple too!

I brought him shed loads of gifts, gold, jewels and spices and he was very gracious although he really had no need of them, being richer than anyone else I know.

I asked him lots of questions, some of them in riddles and he played the game well – he had an answer to them all. He seemed to know everything about everything! I was totally overwhelmed. I've never seen such wisdom and wealth and he claims it is all from his God. Says the Lord his God loves the land and people of Israel so much that he made him a wise king to bring justice and peace.

One of the stories I heard while I was there was about two street women who both had babies about the same time but one of the babies died in the night. Well, one of the mums claimed that the other one had swapped babies but she knew which one was hers and it wasn't the dead one!

So, they came to King Solomon who amazed everyone by asking for a sword and ordered the living baby to be cut in two – and give half to each mum! Well of course the real mum couldn't bear the thought of her baby being killed so said "No, I'll give him up" whilst the other mum thought the order was right – if she couldn't have the child then neither could the other mum. King Solomon then knew the first woman was the real mum and she got her baby back. What wisdom!

After our interesting chats, sumptuous banquets and guided tours of the temple and the city I realised that he was no threat to our land – he had all that he needed. He then gave me presents of things that we can't grow or make and we came home as heavy laden as when we went!

There's lots more to tell you when I next see you – perhaps we can chat about this God of Solomon's – he's really cool.

Regards to your family.

From your loving Cousin 'Queenie'

1 Kings 10

Letter from a Zookeeper
(Daniel in the Lion's Den)

Dear Mum,

You may be wondering why I haven't written for a while. Well, it's because of the strange but amazing things that have been happening here in Mesopotamia.

I'll have to explain the background to this story for you to understand the impact it's had on me, and indeed the king and everyone else here.

Years ago, when we had an influx of captives from the land of Judah in the west, a man called Daniel started rising in the ranks of men who served our king, Darius. Well, apparently, he was so honest and incorruptible that he was made one of three administrators over 120 satraps! We heard that he got his wisdom and abilities from his God and, even though he was about 80 years old, the king wanted to promote him to the highest position in the land! This – an exile – a prisoner even!

Well you can imagine the jealousy and back biting that went on, but no-one could find any weakness or crime regarding Daniel so, it was rumoured, they attacked his religion. These men persuaded King Darius to issue laws and decrees which made himself a god for 30 days and people were only allowed to worship him. His pride and vanity was a big weakness and he really felt top dog with all the people worshipping him as a god.

Unfortunately, Daniel's faith in his God was so strong that he continued to pray to his God three times a day – out loud! Boy was he brave! But of course, he was being watched and so he was taken prisoner and Darius had to punish him, even against his conscience.

So this is where I come in, Mum. Looking after all the lions in the Persian Park, it was my job to keep them hungry so that they could feast on the prisoner. Daniel was put in with the lions but the funny thing was, I couldn't hear any roaring or screaming all night!

I heard from my friend at the palace that Darius was so upset that he didn't sleep at all. I bet he wished he could turn the clock back and stand up for what he really knew was right. I bet he knew his pride and vanity would cost him his peace of mind for evermore.

Anyway, Mum, in the morning we went to see if there was anything left of Daniel's body. I got the lions out of the way and, blow me down – there was Daniel still sitting there on a rock, all in one piece. The king called out to him – maybe he thought he was a ghost – and Daniel answered,

"My God sent his angel and he shut the mouths of the lions. They've not hurt me because I was found innocent in his sight. Nor have I ever done any wrong before you, O King."

Then I had to help lift Daniel out of the lion's den and I could see that he didn't have a mark on him! King Darius was overjoyed but then he suddenly turned angry and had the satraps brought before him and we had to throw them into the den and their wives and children! Oh my goodness what a noise, what a mess, what an outcome. I didn't need to feed my lions for a week after that!

Well, King Darius could see how powerful the God of Daniel was so he ordered that we should all worship this God alone.

And do you know what, Mum, since I've been worshipping this God of Daniel's, I feel like a different person and all sorts of things have been happening. I'll tell you more about the changes in my life when I come to visit you.

Your loving son,

Bacchus

Daniel 6

Letter from a Servant Girl
(Peter's Escape from Prison)

Dearest Mother,

I'm just so bursting to tell you what happened the other day here, where I work, at John Mark's house. Well, his Mum – Mary – and her friends were all having a very intense prayer meeting because firstly, their friend James – son of Zebedee – had been murdered by King Herod and now the chief disciple – Peter – had been locked up ready for a public lynching after Passover.

Well, while they were praying, I heard a knocking at the courtyard door so I went to answer it and heard Peter's voice. Well, I think I might have screamed but, instead of opening it and letting him in, I ran back inside to tell everyone that Peter was there. They didn't believe me at first but eventually went to find him still in the street, knocking away.

We all went crazy with joy and Peter had to calm us all down to tell us how he'd escaped. Apparently, he thought he was dreaming but it was an angel who woke him up, got his handcuffs off, told him to get dressed and follow him. They passed all the guards and the angel opened the gate to the street then left him. (We heard later that about 16 guards were sentenced to death. I bet they wondered how he had done it).

Peter told Mary and the others to tell Jesus' brother James what had happened and then he left. Well, the prayer meeting turned into a real praise party after that.

Wow, what a miracle, Mum! It might be dangerous to be a follower of Jesus but it certainly isn't boring!

Much love,

Rhoda

Acts 12

Introduction to Reflections

I spend a lot of time looking at God's creation (it's the artist in me) and very often I find He speaks to me through it so I have a notebook and pen in my bag.

Sometimes it's just for me, sometimes for someone else or just something to reflect upon.

If I haven't written any Scripture you may like to add what comes to you whilst reading it.

I hope it encourages you to look and listen too.

An Unwelcome Intruder

On my first visit to the orchard in the grounds of an East Sussex retreat, I noticed lots of cow pats and trampled grass which I thought was so incongruous in that beautiful place. Someone mentioned that they thought a bullock had escaped the nearby field and decided the grass was greener in the orchard.

In our spiritual lives the Bible tells us that God has put a hedge around us which even Satan recognises;

"Have you not put a hedge around him and his household and everything he has? You have blessed the work of his hands..." (Job 1: 10)

It's so easy for the devil to mess up our tidy lives and well laid plans if he's allowed access to our innermost places. Once in, he can wreak havoc or at the least make a mess – he needs to be sent packing back to where he belongs and we need to be aware of how easily he can access our minds, those vulnerable areas where he can pop in unbidden.

Ephesians 4: 27 says "...do not give the devil a foothold."

God can be a hedge around us if we're living in obedience to him but in Isaiah 5 v5 he says he can take it away too!

So beware, any weak and unprotected areas are just like an invitation to a wandering bullock!

Blessings

In a hedgerow of brambles and weeds a slight movement proved to be a dull brown butterfly – hardly moving and almost unseen. Suddenly he opened his wings and showed me his brightness – orange, with 'eyes' looking at me. I marvelled at his beauty for an instant but he closed up again. I stood there willing him to 'open up' and show me his markings.

"Don't hide your beauty away. Don't you know you can bless me, just for an instant? You have a gift for blessing others, don't hide it away."

And so, he blessed me again – without him even knowing it.

Do we hide our God-given gifts away? We may not even know we have any gifts or even anything someone else could possibly be blessed by. Sometimes someone smiles at us and makes us feel happy or has manners to let us go first. I've seen someone pay for an item at the check-out when the person in front hadn't got enough money. A phone call or email just to ask how we are is such a blessing, knowing someone cares.

Paul says in Acts 20: 35 that Jesus said "It is more blessed to give than to receive" but it seems to me that it's equally as nice to receive a blessing as to give one.

A Mucky Place

At the back of the big house, I was admiring the pretty flowers, neat lawns and hedges and, looking behind them I saw a septic tank or cesspit! Well of course, in the middle of nowhere they had to have something so it shouldn't have been a surprise.

Then I wondered if we all have somewhere, hidden away, that is full of... muck. I was again reminded of Psalm 139 verses 23-24,

"Search me O God and know my heart... see if there is any offensive way in me"

God alone knows our mucky places. He knows our every thought, our every word before it's on our lips.

The septic tank is a necessary evil but we don't have to have one hidden away in our minds. It may take God some time to dismantle it, even if we are willing but he is the Master of Demolition and can clean us up – that's why Jesus came.

Isaiah 61: 10 says

"I delight greatly in the Lord;
My soul rejoices in my God,
For he has clothed me with garments of salvation
And arrayed me with a robe of righteousness"

I want to swap my cesspit for a robe of righteousness!

God's Pleasures/Our Pleasures

Sitting at the top of Highdown Hill, site of an old iron-age settlement here in Sussex, the landscape was spread out in front of me from far left to far right, along the coast from Brighton to Bognor. – a distance of 40 miles maybe. I think I even saw Culver Cliff on the Isle of Wight.

It was the last of the sunny, warm days in October and it was such a delight to see the green hill sloping down to the Ferring and Goring Gap – the last little bit of green along the built-up Sussex coastline - and the wide seascape beyond. I could see the cars on the roads and the trains on the line and even a white dot on the sea which could have been anything, and I could just make out the Rampion Wind Farm off the coast of Worthing.

As God showed me this vast panorama, I couldn't help thinking of Satan showing Jesus all the kingdoms and trying to tempt him. How futile – they all belonged to him anyway! (Matthew 4: 8-9).

I was so aware that God had created the land for his pleasure and our enjoyment.

Sometimes we have to make an effort to see it (I was puffing quite a bit up that hill and I was trying to fit other things in the day) but it was so restful for my soul and good for me to give thanks and sing;

"Oh Lord my God, when I in awesome wonder consider all the works thy hand hath made,
I see the stars, I hear the mighty thunder, thy power throughout the universe displayed.
When through the woods and forest glades I wander, and hear the birds sing sweetly in the trees;
When I look down from lofty mountain grandeur, and hear the brook and feel the gentle breeze;
Then sings my soul, my Saviour God to thee, how great thou art."

Going Rusty

Walking along a warm and sunny country lane I came across a large gate and behind this was a heap of rusting metal. I could make out four wheels, a spring, a chain and possibly an oil container. Being near a farm I assumed it was once a useful tractor.

I felt sad, thinking of what it once was, imagining it going across fields pulling some implement or other – the remains of which were also there.

It brought me to wonder if I'm going rusty yet – I feel it sometimes, physically on a long walk and sometimes mentally when I can only remember the first letter of the word I need.

The word 'quality' came to mind – what's the quality of my life like at this precise moment? And what about when I'm indoors and it's raining or cold outside? And what about my diary – is it empty or overfull? Do I wish for something different or am I content with what I've got? Am I doing just what I'm meant to be doing? Am I at peace with everything?

Gosh, what a lot of thoughts and questions came from a rusty heap. I looked again and thought,

"I must make the most of the rest of my life and not fritter it away doing unnecessary stuff, stressing out or being bored to tears".

We only have one life on earth and I think being happy in my skin and at peace with God in every circumstance must be my every day goal.

Lifeguards

During the summer months on our beach, we have RNLI lifeguards watching, waiting, on duty just in case someone needs saving from floating out to sea or perhaps drowning.

They are dedicated to observing the actions of those in front of them and are ready to put their own lives at risk to rescue someone.

We are on duty all the time with our friends, neighbours and the total strangers we meet on the bus or in the shops.

If they know Christ, we should be aware of when they are in difficulties and jump in with prayer and practical help.

What about strangers or those we know who don't yet have a relationship with God through Jesus Christ? We should be just as ready and observant to when they have needs.

A comforting word or helpful deed can lead to us rescuing them from an eternity without God. Are we prepared with our testimony? Can we quote gently and appropriately from the living word? Could we lead them to safety if they were 'drowning' and calling out for help?

What a grand thing to rescue someone. How wonderful it is to be rescued!

Nature's Artistry

I love fallen trees because they can fall in all sorts of directions with any number of consequences. On one walk I came across a huge tree that had fallen and its really huge root ball was looking at me so that I could see fifty or a hundred years old gravel and chalk. Next to it I realised was another jagged broken trunk with its bare roots cascading down towards me like a spilt bowl of spaghetti. The soil had been washed away or eroded by so many climbing children so it was truly a beautiful sculpture. (I had to ignore the doggy poo bag that had been left there in front of it!)

When we take the time to just look around us and see beyond the brokenness and destruction there is a beauty and artistry that human minds and hands cannot create.

Unfit for Purpose

My town has 'The Longest Bench' which is comprised of small brightly coloured slats of wood that a lot of local people bought. At one point the 'bench' - which is novel but slightly uncomfortable for anyone with back problems – is 'morphed' into a shelter – again, novel and probably award-winning. However, as any local adult will tell you it is totally impractical for keeping out wind and rain and can only seat a couple of people (again, uncomfortably) but is used as a great climbing frame by anyone under 30!

We were created for a purpose too –

But are we pleasing to God and enjoying him? Are we 'fit for purpose'?

We are only made once so have we 'morphed' into something or wasting our existence? Are we uncomfortable for others to be around?

Our Seeds

I was walking by a hedge of hazel, ash, brambles, giant ferns and nettles taller than me and there was a beautiful yellow honeysuckle probably because seeds had been dropped by a bird, one way or another.

It reminded me of how just a word or deed can sow a seed in someone's life – for either good or bad.

To produce sweet fragrant flowers or luscious fruit it has to be exactly the right seed. We will only be able to sow from what's inside us. We need to be the right flower or fruit that God has made us to be – and we are all unique!

Is it a struggle to sow a seed? Birds just do it without thinking! They just get on with life as they are made for it. I guess we should all be like that.

Filling and Emptying

I have a small device that contains absorbent crystals, and sits on my windowsill soaking up moisture from the air and turning it into water at the bottom, and whenever I want, I can empty it down the sink to get rid of it.

I'm reminded that I can patiently absorb all the irritating things like slow Internet, weeds sprouting up, gardening jobs that I can no longer do or reach, some housework that I don't have the energy for and 'other things' for which I have to keep praying for patience.

But the best thing is that I can take my irritants to God at any time (before it fills up and overwhelms me) and I can just empty it all onto Him.

My crystals of love, joy, peace and patience sometimes run a bit low but, in Christ, there is an endless supply just waiting to fill me up again.

Our Shepherd Leads Us

Looking at all the sheep grazing contentedly in the fields led me to think in a roundabout way to the controversy about Brexit, which reminds me somewhat of the Israelites' exodus out of Egypt.

They didn't have a referendum, of course, they just did what one man (Moses) said that God wanted – what Moses said God was going to do.

Although our country's vote was split nearly in half, I'm sure that there were some of the Israelites who didn't want change – not knowing exactly where they were going, just knowing it might be a hard, long journey. Maybe they thought it was safer to stay where they were, with what they knew. Their overall decision was made because of their faith in God – not so in our day and age.

Whatever we voted for and however our politicians take the country out of the European Union, many people have a sense of insecurity about the future – the unknown. Some feel they are being herded by wolves.

We all have to cope with big and small changes and although we don't know the future, Christians can put their faith in the Good Shepherd who promises to lead us, feed us, comfort us, protect us and see us through to the end. (Psalm 23)

The Israelites took forty years to reach the Promised Land and lots of them grumbled on the way. Moaned about their leader and thought they'd have been better off staying put.

We don't know how long it will take our country to reach stability and economic growth but we each have to trust God with our individual and corporate futures – and what safer hands could we possibly be in!

Pecking Instead of Feasting

Watching a wildlife programme on TV one day there was a vulture on top of a carcass but it was so distracted by other birds around it that it was never going to eat its feast and be satisfied – it could only peck at it.

Our Bible is a feast for our souls but if we only peck at it because we're getting distracted by other things or people, we'll never be satisfied.

Praising too, satisfies our souls, listen to what David wrote in Psalm 63: 3-5:

"Because your love is better than life, my lips will glorify you. I will praise you as long as I live and in your name I will lift up my hands. My soul will be satisfied as with the richest of foods; with singing lips my mouth will praise you."

Let's fill up on his word and thank him with our praises.

Unexpected Delights

Sitting in my parked car recently in an avenue of trees noted for their Autumn colours, the breeze suddenly blew a little harder and there was a wonderful shower of golden yellow leaves all around.

It was early July but because there had been many hot weeks without rain, leaves were falling already – a carpet of them on the straw-coloured grass. Two or three months early and I was treated to an unexpected spectacle of nature.

How often we think things can never change because it's 'always been that way' or 'it's not the right time'.

Let's be open to something different, unusual or new. We could be utterly delighted with it.

Ready for Anything

Sometimes I think I'm over the top when going out or on holiday. I have my 'holiday list' like many others and I think I would regret not using it. When out for the day I check the forecast and perhaps take brolly and mac in case it rains, sun cream in case it's sunny, snack in case I'm hungry, water in case I'm thirsty, notebook, pen etc etc – one heavy bag!

But if a storm does suddenly appear I'm ready for it and smile smugly at all the bedraggled 'unreadies' (how arrogant this sounds.) If the train is very late, I've got my snack (and I do offer to share it – honestly)

But when an unexpected 'squall' hits my personal life I'm not always prepared – my sudden swing of emotions or 'just-bitten-back-outburst' proves that I have weak points where the enemy can slink in.

Sometimes, after an initial uprising of anger, disappointment or frustration I can see what's happening and I can pray in Jesus' name or ask for forgiveness. Sometimes I have to go to the bathroom and sing – somehow praises are a potent weapon. Occasionally a storm floors me so hard that, although I'm aware of it I feel powerless to rise above it. A good friend then comes to my aid and shares her 'brolly' and assures me that the forecast is fine, and stands in the storm with me.

We all need to have 'storm strategies' so we can be ready for almost anything. When the very worst happens that I'm unprepared for and feel utterly powerless I just have to believe that God is 'carrying' me through it just like he promises.

The Bumble Bee

In my garden I saw a big bumble bee really pushing his little head into a flower to get his blessing of nectar. His back was covered in pollen and he looked quite messy but he didn't care. He got his blessing then flew off to spread the pollen elsewhere.

We can receive a blessing from God when we 'dive headfirst' into him – not dithering on the edge and worrying about what might happen to us. We mustn't care if it gets messy – we may dance or burst into song or tongues but we mustn't worry about the consequences of blessings – just be glad God loves us so much to bless us.

When we've been blessed, we take it with us and spread it around. We should be like the bees and pollinate our towns.

The Wind of the Spirit

Walking beside the river one day when the tide was coming in, I saw a white, 2 litre, plastic milk bottle floating on the water but what caught my attention was the fact that, although on its side, it wasn't filling up and sinking and not only that, it was being blown in the opposite direction to the tide!

Sometimes we can unwillingly be blown by a wind from which we feel we can't escape; - addiction, peer pressure, illness etc but God has supernatural power and love, not only to keep us afloat but to help us change direction.

There is so much in the Bible about God's power in the wind and Jesus' power over the elements on Galilee (124 references in my concordance) so he obviously wants us to be aware of it and pray for it.

The Narrow Gate

I grew up in a small village in a railway house next to a level crossing. It really was the road to nowhere and the big gate was only ever opened by the farmer for his small herd of cows.

It was a proper gate that we children would sit on and almost get blown away by the fast London express trains, but next to it was a very narrow pedestrian gate that the hikers and ramblers would use.

We instinctively knew that it was a dangerous place but that was reinforced one day when a cow wandered on to the live rail and got sizzled to death. My memory is of my Dad bravely running up the line waving my Mum's red dress to warn the driver of the oncoming train (long before we had a telephone).

I'm reminded how dangerous it can be to take the wrong path: in Matthew 7: 13 and 14 Jesus tells us to "…enter through the narrow gate for wide is the gate that leads to destruction and many enter through it…" Jesus is that narrow way – the ONE way that leads to life but so many are on the path to destruction and don't want to be told about it.

We are called by Jesus to follow him but we must try to guide others through that narrow gate by our loving words and deeds and when possible – our warnings.

Trapped

I entered the little church through the porch of such rotten wood I was surprised it was still standing. It was musty with age but so full of character. I came across two vases of peonies and, thinking that they were a bit late flowering, I bent to smell them only to realise they were imitation in a vase of water and fresh green vegetation.

Next to me was a buzzing fly. It was in the wrong place, searching for something it wouldn't find. It was probably trapped in the church after it had followed a visitor in the door.

Was it content to remain where it was until it starved to death – uselessly buzzing around achieving nothing? Or would it realise it was trapped and strive with all its strength to find a way out? Would it realise that there was a world out there or was it so used to that musty church it couldn't be bothered? (This is where I started comparing the fly to some people I know!)

What if someone realised that the fly could be free and opened the door for a while – would it stay where it thought it was safe – not realising what freedom would be like? Did it too, think the flowers were real and not see the truth of it?

Oh little fly, you're not meant to be stuck in there. Please look for a way out. I can open the door for you and call you to come but you don't recognise my voice and you stubbornly buzz around frantically – trapped until you die or find the way out.

Vast as the Ocean

One day when I was feeling a little bit overwhelmed by "life" I went for a walk to my local beach, just for the exercise really as I know that relaxes me.

Hardly anyone around, silent except for the surf on the stones and occasional screech of a gull, a bit misty and murky and a bit other-worldly.

Looking at the expanse of water that stretched towards the invisible coast of France, I remembered reading that this was once a land-bridge – there was no English Channel at one time. After the Ice Age the seas gradually rose to make us an island. Climate change has always been with us although whether a land-bridge of plastic will once again join us to the continent is debatable.

I was suddenly aware of the enormous length of eternity – past, present and future – and what a tiny moment I was in and how insignificant I was in the grand scheme of things.

I just love Psalm 104 as it's all about God's wondrous works in creation – verse 25 says "…There is the sea, vast and spacious, teeming with creatures beyond number…"

Yet, even then, I was aware that I was known to God, the author of all Creation. I'm not just a dot in time, I'm a part of his Creation that's important to him.

The whole of Psalm 139 explains how God created us and knows us so well.

I found myself smiling as the parallel thoughts and feelings enveloped me – the enormity and vastness alongside his closeness and significance.

Walking home again by the muddy-looking and fast-flowing River Arun, I felt that everything was back in focus and "life" was easy again. Peace was flowing like a river… over my soul.

On Board Ship

I suffer from motion sickness so I don't go on any ships, boats or floating pontoons unless I have to but my friend has been on many cruises so I hear about life on board.

However, I don't think she's ever talked about the size, shape or look of the ship – it's always the kindness of the crew, the tasty food or the enjoyable entertainment and facilities. It was what went on inside that she remembered and appreciated. She went back again and again because they made her feel good.

In the same way, when we meet someone for the first time, we may be aware of their size, shape or look but it's how they make us feel that's important. It's their kindness, encouragement, attentiveness, caring, listening, trustworthiness and loyalty that ensures we want to meet up with them again.

At a Dementia talk once, the leader said that if a patient is taken out for the day they may not remember where they went or what they ate but they do remember that they were happy

In 1 Samuel 16: 7 it says "Man looks at the outward appearance but God looks at the heart of man."

Beauty fades, waistlines thicken, hair loses its colour but by that time we're pretty much past caring or we realise that beauty is just skin deep anyway and our real friends have a beauty that doesn't fade.

Instructions

When I bought a garden 'companion' seat the person who offered to assemble it said "I don't need to look at the instructions," and felt humbled when he got it wrong.

Years later when I bought another I remembered and thought "I can do it but I need to look at the instructions". I also got it wrong, but having read them several times I got it right in the end.

It reminded me that we all need instructions on how to live our lives because we are all prone to mess up at times. Fortunately we have the Bible to refer to because as it says in Isaiah 53:6, "We all, like sheep, have gone astray, each of us has turned to his own way".

I'm not talking about all the Jewish laws in the Old Testament, although the Ten Commandments are the building blocks for our Christian faith, but Jesus' words on how to obey God and love one another in the New Testament. The disciples' 'Gospels' and Paul's letters reveal what they learned about Jesus' life but also how God guided them by his Holy Spirit as they read their own Scriptures and remembered Jesus' teachings.

So, what's our first instruction?
To love God.

How can we love someone we don't know?
How can we get to know Him?

We get to know God by recognising that He came to earth in the body of Jesus, to die on the cross so that we can be forgiven (if we ask!). He then gives us the free gift of his Holy Spirit so that when we read the Bible, we can understand it! It suddenly becomes personal! We then have a relationship with God which grows as we talk with Him (prayer).

So many people (me included once upon a time) think 'I'm alright, I don't kill, or steal, I'm a nice person,' and never get around to seeing themselves as God sees them. Yes, God loves them – he created them (read Psalm 139), but he wants them to love Him back and be with Him for ever.

With God. it's like we have our 'Instruction Manual' inside us, to refer to at any time, and when we get it wrong, we humble ourselves and say "Sorry, please forgive me".

God allows us to go our own way if we choose to but it can be a lonely, scary and complicated way. Much better to feel loved, forgiven and guided in all we do.

Me First?

Watching the raucous seagulls greedily devouring anything edible, I noticed some hanging back while the dominant ones helped themselves first. Then I thought of the animal kingdom where hierarchy keeps the pack/pride/herd in balance.

Then I thought of humans, similar in many ways – pushing and shoving, selfish ambition, look after number one, me-first culture – or just thoughtlessness?

Once I had to stand in a crowded train for a long time while all the young people sat, engrossed in their music or phones – did they just not see the lady in her seventies, pale and wilting in the aisle, who actually had to ask for a seat in the end?

It does us good to analyse our self-centredness and ambitions – why are we like this? Are we afraid of missing out? Do we crave the attention or admiration of others or the feeling of power when we are in charge or leading something? What is missing in our lives that needs more or better? Do we do certain things just because it gives us a buzz? Is that OK?

Right from childhood we have to be taught to be unselfish – what makes a child (or adult) a bully? It sometimes takes years to find the balance between being a 'doormat' and sticking up for ourselves.

Even the disciples were vying for key positions in Jesus' kingdom (Mark 9: 33-35) and had to learn about servanthood.

Paul wrote "Don't push your way to the front; don't sweet-talk your way to the top. Put yourself aside and help others get ahead. Don't be obsessed with getting your own advantage. Forget yourselves long enough to lend a helping hand". (Philippians 2, The Message).

When we belong to Christ and have that affirmation that we are loved as we are and accepted by Him, known fully by Him (warts and all) then we have no need to prove anything to anyone else, no need to have people approve of us.

Humility takes a long time to learn (and I'm not there yet!) but if you find yourself seeking to be first or loudly demanding your own way, picture the raucous seagulls…

Are You There, God?

Once, when I was travelling in a train, feeling very sorry for myself over something, I was watching the clouds above, which were as gloomy as I felt. I thought about the invisible sun that must be there, but hidden from view, and how I felt at that moment about God not being there for me when I needed Him.

Suddenly, a shaft of sunshine from the dark cloud nearly blinded me, and I chuckled as I believed God was reminding me that, just as the sun was always there, so was He, no matter what I saw or felt. Sure, I believed He was there, but my feelings were overcoming my faith for a moment.

There's a Scripture that says "We fix our eyes not on what is seen, but on what is unseen" (2 Cor 4: 18), just as we "Fix our eyes on Jesus" but see Him by faith.

God has shown me lots of times that He is there and that He hears my thoughts and prayers, but I have to flex my 'faith muscles' continuously to keep them strong.

The longer our relationship goes on, the better we get to know God – the deeper we study the Bible, the further we get to understand Him – the more we talk (pray) to Him, the clearer we see Him acting in our lives – all of which grows our faith.

'Doubting' Thomas wouldn't believe that Jesus had risen from the dead unless he could touch him, and when Jesus appeared to Thomas later and invited him to touch him, Thomas believed. We can't touch Jesus but He said "Blessed are those who have not seen and have yet believed" (John 20: 29) – Jesus calls us blessed!

We may be tempted to beat ourselves up about our doubts, but Jesus understands, and commends us even if our faith is only as big as a tiny mustard seed – which will grow into a huge tree over time!

Consequences

I saw a seagull recently, tearing at a black bin bag that was left out for the dustcart. Someone had used some foil to cook something tasty, and the seagull had pulled it out of the bag and was standing there with a piece of foil in its beak. I wondered if it was just stuck but the gull suddenly swallowed the whole piece – of tin foil!

I reflected as I walked home, how we can be tempted by 'stuff' that's bad for us. When we're young we so want to be like (and be liked by) our peers, that we may go against all that our parents taught us.

The media bombards us with things that promise to satisfy us, make us look glamourous, or be as rich and famous as the latest celebrity.

In the Garden of Eden, Eve was tempted to know as much as God knew (Gen 3)
Jacob deceived his father to get his brother's rightful blessing (Gen 27)
The Prodigal Son's early inheritance went to his head (Luke 15: 11-31)
Samson was tempted by Delilah (Judges 16)
David was tempted by the beautiful Bathsheba (2 Samuel 11)
and many more.

The seagull was just instinctively greedy and couldn't have known the consequences of eating foil – he may have regurgitated it but he could have had a horrible death.

We instinctively know there are consequences if we do wrong but temptation is often stronger than instinct or warnings.

By reading the Bible we can learn of others' mistakes and we can learn how to avoid them and their consequences. We can read about Jesus who sympathises with us, and was tempted too (Hebrew 2: 18 and Hebrews 4: 15-16), and we have a God, who wants to helps us. (1 Cor 10: 13).

The Field of Lavender

On a visit to a lavender farm, I found myself surrounded, thigh-deep in stunning purple fragrance.

Each single plant had been lined up in rows to enable people and machines to admire, weed or harvest at just the right time.

Every little aromatic bush had dozens of bees and hoverflies, and each little creature was making a tiny noise.

However, all of the plants and all of the creatures, put together en masse, made a sight and sound that was awe-inspiring – it had the WOW factor.

It suddenly reminded me of when Christians gather together to praise and worship with grateful and glad hearts. On our own we may not bother, or we may be out of tune, or feel insignificant but, together, – well!

Sometimes we feel as if angels are singing with us, often our hearts are fit to burst.

Is that how the bees feel, gorging on 'purple pollen'?

Is our God bending His ear to listen, to enjoy our fragrance?

I don't think I'll be singing again without thinking of that beautiful lavender and those busy little bees!

The Lorryload of Blessing

Amongst the fumes of traffic, under the flight path of a Gatwick-bound jet, and amid the concrete, brick and metal, came a big lorry carrying dozens of huge sawn trees – giant logs.

Suddenly the wonderful smell of the countryside – and saw mill – filled my nostrils and transported me for a few seconds out of the busy, noisy, dirty, high street, to the world of nature, even to the woods of my childhood.

It was such a momentary blessing – not quite seeing heaven in the midst of hell – but reminding me that blessings and surprises can come at any time and in any place. I wasn't seeking out that lorry, I wasn't even waiting for a blessing, it was just a little gift in my walk with God – like He lifted me up into His arms and put me down again – (it doesn't take much to please me). Did anyone else see or smell those logs? They were there for all to see if people weren't looking down at the ground or in a shop window or at their phones.

In 2 Corinthians 2: 15-16 Paul says Christians are the pleasing aroma of Christ – an aroma that brings life.

So, we can be a blessing from God.

How can we give someone a little gift of kindness that will brighten their day and maybe bring a smile? Look up from the floor – look around – a prayer of blessing for someone walking by – or flying overhead in an aeroplane – may enable God to open their eyes to something heavenly!

Tuning In

Walking alone, through a very quiet wood one day, I stopped to listen to a noisy woodpecker somewhere above me. I perched myself on a fallen tree trunk then realised I should turn my hearing aid up to 'surround sound', and I was startled to hear dozens and dozens of other birds, hidden away, all chirruping loudly – it wasn't a quiet wood after all!

It made me think of how we can all be unaware of what is going on around us. We're thinking about what's happened or what may happen – planning, questioning, worrying – just life really.

What will you hear or see if you make a concerted effort to 'tune in' to what's going on around you? – now there's a challenge!

In the garden or countryside, it may be a flower, bird or animal that surprises and delights you – in a town centre it may be a beautiful building, or a person who you could encourage, compliment or comfort.

It may be that, in the stillness and quietness God will nudge you, guide you, speak to you, encourage you or comfort you.

Many Psalms are attributed to David who looked around him and observed creation whilst pouring his heart out to God.

The disciples listened to Jesus and observed his ways and were able to pass it on to us.

Scientists, doctors etc, all have to 'think outside the box' and be aware of other possibilities.

Sometimes we all need to stop, look, listen and think.

The Lone Sheep

Looking at a Facebook post called Rush Hour in Ireland, it showed a solitary sheep walking down an empty street, only to be confronted by a whole flock running towards him. It spun him round and carried it with them down the street.

After laughing, I didn't know whether to be pleased that it was no longer alone or concerned that it was being taken along against its will. The lone sheep was obviously shocked by the sight in front of him but it could have got out of their way or hidden behind a car.

It made me ponder on how easy it is for us humans to be swayed/carried along by popular opinions/culture etc, either because we don't want to be a 'lone voice' or we aren't aware how we can be prepared/protected.

We can be extreme 'hermits' or we can be very uncomfortable on our own or somewhere in the middle but we all have a mind and a choice.

As we age, we normally think of ourselves as no longer naïve or gullible, but a lot of older people can still be 'conned' into something if they are not on their guard.

2 Peter 3: 17 says "Be on your guard so you may not be carried away by the error of lawless men…"

James tells us to guard our tongues and Paul says in 1 Cor 16 :13, Acts 20 :31 and Luke 12 :15 to be on our guard.

It says in Philippians that if we thank the Lord and pray to Him, the peace of God will guard our hearts and minds.

Whether it be in politics, religion, peer pressure or addictions, the lure of 'the world' can be very strong and we need to always be alert and aware of what could sweep us along with it.

Finally, in John 10, Jesus talks about Him being the gate for the sheep pen. When the wolf comes, Jesus is there guarding us vulnerable ones. He's there in front of us, aware of what's coming. He cares for us and won't abandon us and run away.

Let's hide ourselves in Jesus' sheep pen and not be afraid.

Trusting

I was watching two wet-suited amateur surfers off my local beach – one was laying on his board using his arms and the other was standing using a paddle. What if their arms got tired or they lost the paddle? They would be at the mercy of the tide, current and wind and could have drifted way out to sea and, being February, there were no lifeguards watching them through binoculars. They were both trusting in their own strength.

We take risks all the time and rely on the flimsiest of things to get us through our lives – education, money, car, health, family and we trust that we don't lose these things, whilst knowing that we might.

In the Bible God is called our strength, rock, fortress, deliverer and shield. (Psalm 18) and (in Hebrews 6 :19) He's our firm and secure anchor for our souls.

Proverbs 18: 10 says "the name of the Lord is a strong tower; the righteous run to it and are saved"

In Hebrews 4 :12 we have His living and active word (Scriptures) which is sharper than any double-edged sword, and Ephesians 6 says we can put on the whole armour of God.

In my weaker moments when I've been almost penniless, unwell or feeling very sorry for myself, these words have reminded me that I'm not quite at rock-bottom – He is there for me, strong and mighty; He cares, He comforts and He often leads me to the quiet waters (Psalm 23) that I'm so desperate for, and stops me 'drifting out to sea without a paddle'.

Rejection

When I was at school, I was a shy and mediocre student and was sometimes overlooked by teachers and wasn't in a "popular girl's" group. As a teenager I found it hard to be 'dumped' by a boy for a prettier or cleverer girl (well that's what I thought they were). In my first marriage I was betrayed for someone who had a quality that I didn't have (or want).

I've seen most of my family rejected by partners who wanted someone 'better', 'different' or 'more fulfilling'. I've seen friends with obvious talents passed over by leaders or bosses who believed they knew best.

In my generation, there were no 'snowflakes' – we may not have liked it but we just got on with our lives. Our disappointments fashioned our characters and probably made us stronger and able to accept that it's all part of life, although I know there are some unfortunate casualties who never manage to get 'repaired'.

In the Bible we read of so many who were passed over, rejected or betrayed – think of Hagar (Genesis 16 and 21), Leah (Genesis 29 and 30), Esau (Genesis 27) Joseph (Genesis 37) and David's older brothers (1 Samuel 16). I wonder how the obscure Joseph Barsabbas, also known as Justas, felt when Matthias was chosen over him to be the 12th apostle (Acts 1: 23-26). Then Jesus – misunderstood, betrayed, mistreated, rejected and murdered!

Why should we expect life to be ideal? – Other people to be perfect? Our lives can be wonderful and they can be rubbish. However, because Jesus has been through it and God is with us in it, we can take enormous comfort in knowing we are in his hands. We may suffer consequences of our stupid mistakes and others' sinful actions, but Immanuel – God with us – knows the outcome – he's written the end of the book!

Just as parents have to let their children make mistakes and suffer hardships in order to mature, so our heavenly Father watches over us while we go through 'stuff', and if we look for and ask for strength, comfort and healing love, we'll find One who never lets us down.

Running to God

When one of my granddaughters was a toddler, I had the happy task of collecting her from nursery school one day a week and get to know her for a few hours.

Sometimes she would be asleep on the floor and I had to gently wake her up and ease her floppy body into her coat. At the beginning she always looked like a frightened rabbit until she realised who I was.

Gradually, as she saw more and more of me, she came to trust me and knew that she would be safe with me, and one day she ran across the room into my wide open arms calling out "Gran, Gran."

What pleasure that gave me and what a surge of love I had for her – she never knew how much!

When I talk to God, I often remember those feelings and know that I can "bother him" as many times that I wish and he will always be pleased and love me more than I could ever know. If I am anxious, I know he is a safe place to run to.

Proverbs 18: 10 says "The name of the Lord is a strong tower; the righteous run into it and are safe."

We may be like that timid toddler at first but as we get to know God better, we will be aware of his presence and can run to him for any reason or none!

Mark 10: 16 says "Jesus took the children into his arms, put his hands on them and blessed them."

Tears

I was watching a raindrop slowly and quietly run down the window and it reminded me of seeing a tear creep down someone's cheek. When the rain got heavier and it joined all the drops to pour noisily down the window I got to thinking about the different ways and reasons that we cry.

How many of us have lain on the floor in physical agony, wetting the carpet with our tears of pain and frustration?

Who has silently wept into their pillow tears of grief, loss, betrayal or self-pity?

Have you been 'holding it all together' only for someone to be kind, and their arm around your shoulder breaks the dam and you sob loudly and uncontrollably into their sympathetic armpit?

I'm sure everyone has snuffled or blubbered into their hankies while watching something emotional on TV.

I love the way the Bible doesn't relate crying just with women –

In Psalm 6: 6 even David says "I am worn out from groaning: All night long I flood my bed with weeping and drench my couch with tears" and we understand from Psalm 56: 8 that God records our tears and keeps them in his 'bottle'.

Famously, Jesus wept. All around were weeping and wailing because Lazarus had died and I wonder how he joined in – standing up and hugging them or crouching down and wiping his eyes on his sleeve? He knew something the others didn't but he wept along with them.

All through our lives God has been there with us, shared our sorrow and grief, seen and heard just what it was that brought us to that point, and often brings comfort in beautiful ways. Weeping's not weakness – we were created with emotions but, as Solomon said "There's a time to weep and a time to laugh". We need both!

Faithfulness

It always delights me when spring flowers emerge from the dark earth, and new buds and shoots appear on bare branches. What a wonder when chicks break out from hard shells and baby creatures are born just in time for the warmer weather.

How comforting is that warm sun on our faces and that feeling that something nice is coming soon.

This has been happening for so long because our God is faithful.

Psalm 111 says "…Great are the works of the Lord; they are pondered by all who delight in them….the works of his hands are faithful and just…"

And he promises that it will always be like this –

In Genesis 8: 22 it says "As long as the earth endures, seed time and harvest, cold and heat, summer and winter, day and night will never cease."

He promises that he will never abandon us –

In Matthew 28: 20 he says "And surely I am with you always, to the very end of the age."

He promises to forgive us if we are truly sorry –

1 John 1: 9 says "He is faithful and just and will forgive us our sins and purify us from all unrighteousness."

And when our time on earth is over, Jesus promised that, if we belong to him, he will take us to be with him (John 14: 1-4.)

What a faithful God.

The Six-Foot Hedgehog

Whilst driving home from a prayer meeting in my home town in the dark I rounded a bend and there was a six-foot hedgehog dancing in the road in my headlights! He jumped on to the pavement and as I passed it, I could see in my rear-view mirror that he had sparkly lights on his waistcoat! I laughed fit to burst as I realised it was Hampton, a person dressed up, our local mascot.

Suddenly the words "Expect the Unexpected" came into my mind and I thought about the prayers for healing that I had just been praying and I thought 'how can we expect the unexpected when we don't know what the unexpected is?' Maybe it means 'be on the alert' or 'believe for the impossible'.

When John was baptising and preaching repentance, the people were waiting expectantly and were all wondering in their hearts if John might be the Christ (Luke 3: 15) – people were expecting a Messiah but Jesus wasn't what they were expecting.

The angel told Mary about Elizabeth being six months pregnant "For nothing is impossible with God" (Luke 1: 37) and Jesus said in Matt 19: 26 "With God all things are possible."

I think God is encouraging us to expect him to do great things – we can believe for the impossible.

The Rescue

The news on the radio said that a man had died in Thailand trying to help save a crowd of boys who had been trapped for two weeks in an underground cave.

The man had been taking oxygen tanks to the boys but apparently had run out of air himself on the way back.

This brave man gave his life for these boys but he didn't die willingly or knowingly. "Very rarely will anyone die for a righteous man though for a good man someone might possibly dare to die" said Paul (Romans 5: 7), but Jesus did – he knew he would be killed and he could have got out of it but to rescue us he had to do it and he did it for the unrighteous and evil.

Those boys will be eternally grateful to that hero and I hope it will change their lives somewhat but when we are saved by Jesus our lives are changed radically for ever even past our own death.

What a rescue that is!

Support

Walking up a narrow country lane with sheep bleating in the nearby field and the brown butterflies fluttering amongst the kerbside vegetation, my eyes were arrested by an old oak tree covered in ivy, which had a broken branch hanging, but supported by many tendrils of bright green ivy.

I was trying to decide if the ivy was a clinging pest or a helpful companion but then decided it didn't matter as the ivy was wrapped around the broken branch protecting it and preventing it from falling.

We too, sometimes need someone who will be there for us when we are breaking or falling – someone who will hold us and support us. It might be someone who we once regarded as a bit clingy or someone who has been a dear friend for a long time but in our time of need it's how they react that's important.

We may need our 'ivy' one day or we may be called to be a support. Let's hope we are not seen as a pest!

Riding the Thermals

Whilst sitting in the garden a seagull overhead wheeled past me noisily and as I continued to look upwards, I saw another bird, possibly a buzzard, going around in circles getting higher and higher. It wasn't flapping its wings at all, just calmly riding the thermals and taking advantage of a natural event. I watched it for ages as it got so high it was just a dot that touched the clouds and disappeared.

When we tap into God's provisions, we too can be unflappable and 'ride the thermals' or even 'ride the storms' of life. It takes practice and sometimes a bit of concentration (just taking time out with prayer and Scripture) but it is possible to be in that place of 'the peace that transcends all understanding' (Philippians 4: 7) and afterwards know that we have been supernaturally uplifted by God. It's not a question of 'trying' but praying for help and seeing the results.

There's so much in the Bible about being lifted and carried on eagles' wings or riding on the wings of the wind and each quotation reminds us of how much God wants to lift us up to heavenly places.

Picking Up Splinters

Many years ago, a ship sank off our South Coast and huge piles of wood were washed up on miles of beaches.

Big machines were used to push the heaps of timber near to the promenades so that they could be carried away by lorry but there were also some men on the beach bending over and picking up the tinier pieces and putting them into black bags. A lady behind me said to her husband "That's a waste of time, there must be millions of splinters there."

I wondered if the men were thinking "What good is it picking up a few splinters among these millions?" but I got to thinking about the things we do or say that feels like a 'drop in the ocean' or a 'splinter in a million' – the small donations to charity that, together, make up several thousands of pounds; the letter to our MP that may change his way of voting in Parliament; the word in season that eventually brings someone into the kingdom of Christ.

In the parable of the talents (Matt 25: 23) Jesus says "Well done, good and faithful servant! You have been faithful with a few things; I will put you in charge of many things"

What do we feel is a waste of time or a drop in the ocean or a splinter in a million? Maybe God see things differently.

Overgrown

Walking somewhere I hadn't been for seven or eight years I was struck by the way it had changed. From open and sunny pathways, it was so overgrown I could hardly see the lake below me. I felt sad about the change and the amount of shade but then I focussed on the range of wild flowers, butterflies and number of birds darting about.

As we age our bodies change even if our minds still feel young. We may even look a bit overgrown but, instead of looking at wrinkles, lines and greying hair etc, think of what else we have.

Maybe we have the wisdom of experience, memories, a different attitude to the impetuousness, rashness and even arrogance of youth. Maybe more patience with others even though we get impatient with our own weaknesses. Maybe an understanding that some things aren't always black and white (tolerance?) and aren't always what they seem to be at first glance – that there may be an unseen reason why other people are 'different' or 'awkward'. What is perfect anyway?

Let's focus on the positive and shrug off change or disappointment as much as possible.

No One's Useless

Wandering around an orchard I came across an old dead tree, still standing – well, leaning at quite an angle and resting on four branches like an old man doing press ups. Looking at it closely I have to touch the beautifully lined, cracked and wrinkled bark. The colours and texture are rather unusual and I'm thinking 'How can something so obviously dead look so interesting?'

Clambering all over it is a white rambling rose like a misty wedding veil on Miss Haversham's old head.

This tree is not so useless after all – it is beautiful in its own way and what is left is being used.

When we die, we leave mementos behind and some leave written works that are read for centuries or songs or pieces of art. Great-grandmother's jewellery and Grandfather's war memorabilia will be handed down to future generations with a story attached.

What are our footprints in this life? Someone once said that people may not remember what you said or did but they will remember how it made them feel.

That's worth pondering on.

No one's death need to be wasted.

No One's Hidden

Outside my window on holiday, in a disused corner, behind a summer house, log pile, water butt, roller, and two wheelbarrows – so, only seen by me, out of the window – was a beautiful collection of foxgloves – some eight or ten feet tall, rambling roses, oxeye daisies and dangerous-looking red berries of the cuckoo pint or wild arum. What a hidden away collection – attracting all the local insects and pollinating creatures.

We can sometimes feel hidden away – neglected, ignored, useless, no longer in the spotlight, no longer 'in the front row'. God, however, always knows where we are, sees us and always has a use for us, whether we are encouraging friends, talking to visitors, writing letters (or emails) or praying for loved ones or just 'being' – in a relationship with him that he appreciates and enjoys. Just think, even if we only had our mind left, we can still please God!

In Jeremiah 23 :24 God asks "Who can hide in secret places so that I cannot see them?" He sees all, whatever is hidden, wherever we are – to me that is a comforting encouragement.

Maintenance

Whilst eating in cafes or staying in guest houses my eyes somehow spot the cobwebs, peeling paint or frayed carpets and I wonder how many café and guest house owners eat, sit or lay in the places that their customers have to.

Once, these places were brand new or newly refurbished but they haven't been maintained and they have lost their freshness. Maybe the owners are too busy or have stopped caring.

We were newly born once and as we age it's easy to 'let ourselves go'. Even if we are born-again, we can let ourselves slip spiritually by going to church less, reading the Bible less, praying less or meeting our Christian friends less until we are like a cold ember fallen out of the fire.

We need to 'maintain' ourselves – check up on ourselves. Does God see us lose our freshness? Have we stopped caring? Maybe we need to do a regular 'maintenance check' – physically and spiritually – and bring back that newly-born freshness.

Imitators

Looking at some swans one early Summer day I saw a tiny cygnet with stubby little brown wings trying to imitate its parent who was arching up out of the water flapping its huge wings. I laughed but it was the only way for the little one to learn.

As children we naturally imitate our parents, as teens we imitate anyone who we aspire to be like, sometimes with disastrous results.

Paul tells us in Ephesians 5: 1 to be imitators of God and live a life of love, just as Christ loved us… That love goes beyond affection to self-sacrificing service.

Paul also tells us in 1 Cor 4: 16 to imitate him as 'their father through the gospel.' He was able to say that because he walked close to God, spent time in the word and prayer and was aware of God's presence in his life at all times. God was Paul's example, therefore Paul's life could be an example to other Christians.

Later I saw some cygnets almost fully grown with just a few brown feathers and they were flapping as good as their parents. They had learned just by example.

We try to be imitators of the Lord but we often fail, as we are all a work in progress but Jesus came to show us what we should aspire to become and he provides the grace to help us to do our best.

Fruity Blessings

One day I felt compelled to drive to a specific place in the countryside and I wondered what God might be going to say to me or show me.

I wondered around enjoying God's presence, the autumn colours, reeds by the river, berries on the bushes but not 'arrested' by anything in particular but just as I turned back, I came across a box of apples by the side of the road – how come I didn't see them before?

My apple tree had produced hardly any fruit that year but someone here had an abundance and I just felt so blessed as I put a few in my handy carrier bag.

There's a line in Song of Solomon 7: 8 that says "…the fragrance of your breath like apples…" and I felt that God and I had just been out for a lovely companionable walk of blessings.

Changing Direction

Looking up at the sky from my garden on the South Coast of England I see a lot of planes with their white contrails going in different directions.

Mostly they go in straight lines and I try to guess where they might be heading but one day, when I couldn't even see the distant plane the contrail suddenly 'bent' at a 90-degree angle and I thought "It's probably going to Paris" but why the sudden change of direction? The pilot already knew where he was heading didn't he? Was it something to do with the 'plane corridors'? Was there an emergency on board?

We may have rigid plans and know where we're heading but we need to be ready to change direction if God shows us clearly that we're off course.

Sometimes we have a choice and we need to take time to pray and ask God for the right direction and if we don't hear that still, small voice we have to take one path and pray God will stop us if it's wrong. (I don't believe God has a Plan B, he sees us if we go wrong and uses it.)

Sometimes we can get stopped in our tracks – maybe losing our job or our health – and we are unable to go straight on. We need to try to embrace the situation – after all, our ways are in God's hands – and ask where we should be going next and what are we meant to do in the meantime. Often he just says "Rest awhile".

Sometimes we know where we're going but our journey just needs a tweak, an adjustment, to get us where we're meant to be. I'm so glad God knows where we'll end up!

"For I know the plans I have for you", declares the Lord, "plans to prosper you and not to harm you, plans to give you hope and a future." (Jeremiah 29: 11)

A Safe Place

At the bottom of the orchard next to where I was staying on holiday was a round area of about sixty saplings in three quarters of a circle. There were seats for about a dozen people and a fire pit in the centre with the charred remains of the latest bonfire. It felt very sheltered although any wind could come through but there was no wind, just dappled shade so even if the sun and wind were strong, they couldn't harm me. A child could slip through the gaps but there were only squirrels and rabbits there and birds twittering their little heads off and a blackbird hopping just metres away.

Why did I feel so secure there? It was as if God had got his arms around me and I was reminded of the words I heard that morning, "You hem me in – behind and before" (Psalm 139 :5).

I enjoy being free, in the open air with the wind blowing around me – it's exhilarating, but I felt so safe and secure in that secret place. It reminded me again of the words that morning,

"My frame was not hidden from you when I was made in the secret place. When I was woven together in the depths of the earth, your eyes saw my unformed body." (Psalm 139 :15-16)

Was it that early enclosed place that made me feel secure or was it because God was there, could see me, knew my every thought and loved me more than I could ever understand?

It wasn't a tidy place there – the yellowing leaves were covering the grass and the wooden bench was smothered in lichen and each chair had a cushion of yellow leaves upon it. God doesn't need a tidy place or an intelligent mind or a perfect body – he just wraps himself around us and loves us as we are, and, if we just realised this wherever we are we'll know we are in a safe and secure place in him.

A Right Perspective

From ground level the lake was bright and shiny and I couldn't see any fish so it looked rather uninspiring and nondescript.

However, walking up a nearby hill I could see into its clear depths with fish, reeds and weeds – I had a completely different perspective from on high.

God sees into our very depths, knows what's there and loves us anyway. When life gets a bit much and we go through all sorts of trials maybe we need God's higher perspective – it could change our viewpoint in more ways than one.

The whole of Psalm 139 lets us know how God sees us and verses 15 and 16 tells us that we were not even hidden from him in our mothers' wombs.

The Little Lamb

The Bible often talks about Jesus being the sacrificial lamb but it also speaks of mankind as lost sheep, (Luke 15: 3-7) and sheep that have gone astray (Isaiah 53: 6)

I recently came upon a statue of a man holding a lamb under his right arm. With his left hand he was holding the lamb's head against his chest, over his heart. The man also had his head down so that his chin was resting on the lamb's head, as if he was whispering to him.

That lamb looked so comfortable, so close to his owner, so loved by him, that, for a moment, I envied him - until I realised that I already have that position with Christ.

If we have committed our lives to Jesus, the Christ;

- We are already being carried by him (Isaiah 40: 11)
- We can hear his voice if we stay close to him (John 10: 3-4, 27)
- We can know we are loved extravagantly (Eph 3: 14-21)
- Jesus has the power to protect us from the wolf (John 10: 11-13)

Sometimes when I get a bit overwhelmed with life, I imagine Jesus holding me, listening to my bleating, and I receive comfort and peace that he has everything under control (Isaiah 26: 3)

Not the Gardener

I've written a few times about expecting the unexpected and looking out for surprises However, I was caught out myself whilst wandering around the gardens and parklands of a conference centre situated in the grounds of a lovely country house.

I was admiring a beautiful white Philadelphus when a man appeared and we chatted about the lovely plants and topiary. I casually asked "Are you the gardener here?" to which he replied "No, I live here" – he was the owner of the big house, and we continued chatting about his overgrown pond.

As I looked closer at his clothes, I felt a bit silly as they obviously weren't gardeners' attire.

I immediately thought of Mary Magdalene at the garden tomb (John 20: 10-18) She hadn't even recognised the two men in the tomb as angels and when she turned around, she was so distraught because Jesus' body wasn't there, that she didn't recognise the man she'd known for some time. She thought he was the gardener until he spoke her name.

I wonder if we would recognise Jesus or an angel unless they spoke our name?

All The World's A Stage

An author wrote a play. It was a beautiful play, with a beginning and an end. He was an architect too so he constructed the theatre. He was a carpenter and painter so he made the stage and all the props. He created actors and actresses – made them miniatures of himself. He wrote the script and gave each player a copy saying,

"I want you to enjoy yourselves in this play, so follow the script and you'll be really happy and everything will be perfect."

But right from the start those players rebelled against the script. There was discord and arguments.

"The author favours you more than me – I'll get rid of you mate!"

"He's made you a king – I wanna be a king!"

"I don't agree with this script – I'm gonna change it!"

Some didn't even bother with the script – they just did what they pleased and of course it was utter chaos.

There were some who tried to please the author by following the script and he was very pleased with them even though they fluffed their lines and missed cues but so many were doing their own thing that the author decided to speak to them firmly. Still the majority wouldn't listen so he thought

"The only way is to get down on that stage myself and tell them where they're going wrong."

However, because he was so big, just part of him went down among the players. He looked like them so he merged in well and started talking to them about the mess they were making of the play. He told them about the author and how sad he was because he loved those players and wanted them to be really happy. He moved about all over the stage and told them that if they believed that he WAS the author and if they were sorry they'd been rebellious, one day, when they'd finished their part in the play, they would be able to go and live with the author for ever and they'd never be unhappy again. However, if they chose to ignore him and carry on doing their own thing, when the curtain came down for them they would be thrown into the orchestra pit where it was dark and noisy.

He caused quite a stir among the players. Some said,

"How dare he tell us we're wrong! We read out every line meticulously – especially the punctuation marks! Our noses are almost glued to the pages. We've learnt it all off by heart too!"

Others said,

"Wow! What he says makes sense. I never realised I was missing half the lines out and altering others to suit myself."

The he said,

"I've got to go now but listen, the author knows that it's not easy to follow the script but if you tell him you really want to please him and you ask him to help you, he'll put something inside you that's like a little two-way radio. You see, you can whisper to the author and he'll hear you but because of all this racket that's going on down here and all the distractions, you can't hear his voice properly but with this device you leave it switched on and you can talk to each other any time you like."

Then before he could say much more some people came and trussed him up like a chicken and threw him into the orchestra pit. However, to the delight of his friends and the consternation of his enemies, all the chains fell off and he rose up, soared over the top of them all to where the author was looking on and sat down in the director's chair on the author's right hand side and waited to see what would happen. Well, as the play progressed, amazing things began to happen. Those who believed switched on their two-way radio…

"Er – excuse me Sir-er – can you hear me?"

"Of course I can hear you my beloved and if you stay tuned in we can talk to each other as often as you wish. I want to help you with your script and tell you if you go wrong. I want you to enjoy yourself, and if you want to sing songs to me, I'd really enjoy that too."

"Wow! This really blows my mind. I'm going to tell all my friends."

Well, some just didn't want to know - "Crazy people – fancy falling in love with the author."

Others were downright hostile - "Lock them up, beat them up, they're spoiling our script."

Many didn't know what they were talking about so the author spoke into the two-way radio and said to the believers;

"You'd better add a bit more on to my script and that'll give everybody a chance to get to know me. I'll give you the words – you just write them down."

So the script became a bit bigger and more and more players discovered their two-way radio. However, the sad thing was, many thought they didn't need the new part of the script -

"We agree with all the old lines of course, we don't do anyone any harm, we're fine as we are thanks. I'm a good person, of course I'll meet the author."

Some read the script but didn't know about the switch. The radio was there in them but they didn't know they had to switch on, speak - and listen, they just sat back and wondered why they were still struggling on alone.

Some knew about the switch but were scared - "What if he tells me to do something that looks a bit silly? What if I get taken over completely? Some of my friends are waving their hands in the air, some are even dancing! I don't want that to happen to me, I'll lose all my friends, besides, I'm too ladylike! Goodness he might tell me to go and hug my grumpy old neighbour!"

Quite a lot thought they had switched on and because they weren't getting any response, they got a bit bored. They kept up the pretence of being in touch with the author simply because it had become a habit and, besides, in some circles it had become the done thing. Many were quite clever at reciting things off by heart like 'Thy kingdom come thy will be done' whilst mentally deciding what they would be doing later or when they should put their dinner on. Most didn't realise they were missing out on the communication bit.

Some, however, were hungry to hear the author's voice, some were lonely, some were sick, some realised they needed the author's help to get their part right. They bumped into a little group of believers who were switched on and noticed the difference.

"Hey – they're not worrying quite so much as us. Why are they so happy – they act as if they're in love! The author actually spoke to them? How can we know more about this?"

So they met with them, talked with them, learnt how to switch on and communicated with their author. They suddenly realised what they'd been missing – they could now understand the script better, the part they had to play was underlined, if they found it hard going, well, they just told the author and he helped them. Even in the noisy scenes they could still hear his voice but quite often they found a quiet corner, meditated on their script and the author would whisper gently to them.

On one side of the stage there was a giant bookcase stacked high with scripts – some had hard covers with gold letters embossed on them, some were tatty and torn, some were written differently but they all said the same thing inside.

Close by were lots of actors and actresses having a whale of a time – but with no scripts:

"We don't need a script, we're having more fun without it. Who cares what the author thinks, I'm making up my own lines. I've heard his lines are boring – they say it's don't do this and don't do that. Anyway who wants to go and live with the author, he's probably as boring as his old scripts. I'm not even sure there is an author – has anyone ever seen him? And look at the state of this theatre! Why doesn't he do something about it? Oh excuse me, my mates are calling me, we're off to take pot-shots at the light bulbs then we're going to duff up some of those stupid believers – they don't fight back you know! Have a word with those eggheads over there, the ones making fireworks - don't touch any buttons though, one of them is set to blow the whole theatre to bits", and off he went to find new thrills.

Over the other side of the stage the players were different – red, yellow, black, brown – speaking differently, dressed differently, but not many had scripts. They looked longingly over to the large bookcase. Occasionally a believer would bring over a small box of scripts and share them out, some only having a page or two – and amazing things happened – they discovered their two-way radio. They didn't hesitate to switch on and great hordes of players started communicating with the author. He spoke to anyone – anyone who wanted him – it didn't matter which side of the stage they were on.

Hey – wait a minute – what's happening? We're on the stage too. We're not the audience – we're part of that play. It's had a long run, we'd better be ready for the final curtain. Where's my script? Have you got yours? Yes but have you read it? Are your words underlined or is it a jumble? Whereabouts on the stage should you be? Do you know about the two-way radio? Have you actually got one? Have you switched it on?

Player to author – come in please.

(I read this out on a stage in 1984!)

Other Publication by this Author

All Sorts of Thoughts
Poetry and Prose